ALPINE
SKI MAINTENANCE AND REPAIR

ALPINE

SKI MAINTENANCE AND REPAIR

SETH MASIA

CONTEMPORARY BOOKS

A TRIBUNE NEW MEDIA/EDUCATION COMPANY

Library of Congress Cataloging-in-Publication Data

Masia, Seth.
    Alpine ski maintenance and repair.

    Rev. ed. of: The ski maintenance and repair handbook.
c1982.
    1. Skis and skiing—Equipment and supplies—Maintenance
and repair.   I. Masia, Seth. Ski maintenance and repair
handbook.   II. Title.
GV854.9.E6M37   1987   688.7′693   87-9236
ISBN 0-8092-4718-6

Published by Contemporary Books, Inc.
Two Prudential Plaza, Chicago, Illinois 60601-6790
Manufactured in the United States of America
International Standard Book Number: 0-8092-4718-6

Contents

PART IV: POLES AND GOGGLES

Preface

It was easy to write the first edition of *The Ski Maintenance and Repair Handbook*, which was published in 1982. I simply rewrote some of my "Workbench" columns from *SKI Magazine*. The column appears whenever I learn something new about ski tuning or ski equipment care. Since 1982, the ski factories have learned a great deal about making skis go faster, turn easier, and last longer, and both boots and bindings have changed in important ways, also. The revised edition addresses all of these changes.

Two very important changes have occurred in ski making. First, ski-makers are using much harder, tougher forms of polyethylene plastics on the bottoms of most high-performance skis than they used to. These sintered plastics are not only more durable, but significantly faster than traditional extruded grades of polyethylene. The sintered plastics are, in all ways, an improvement over preceding base materials, but because they are harder, they are more difficult to file and grind to shape, and also more difficult to patch once damaged. As a result, most ski shops that do a high-volume business in ski repair have installed very sophisticated and highly automated machinery designed specifically for tuning sintered-base skis.

The machines for this work—generally called *stonegrinders*—are very expensive. A typical stonegrinder sells for about $17,000 in 1987. Naturally, the machines cost too much for most skiers, even for coaches and other ski pros who tune a lot of skis. They have had to learn how to repair and tune sintered bases by hand, and it has taken several years for the real professionals—the racer-chasers who hand file and wax skis for World Cup and Olympic teams—to give up the secrets of tuning sintered bases by hand for ultimate speed.

It turns out that the secrets are remarkably simple. With hand tools you can buy in any hardware store, a skier armed with a little common sense and a sensitive touch can produce a World Cup-quality ski base. And that's the second important development in ski making: manufacturers have learned that structure is important in ski base performance.

When ski tuners use the word *structure* they refer to the texture of the base. The slickest, quickest ski base is not, as previously believed, a perfectly smooth, mirrorlike surface, but one with hundreds of microscopic striations running along the length of the ski. These striations help break up surface tension in the thin film of water under the ski base, channeling in air and ducting off water like the fine treads in a racing car's rain tires.

Most of the experimentation to find the right way to develop a ski base structure was done by technicians at the Austrian ski factories, notably Fischer, Atomic, and Head, by chemists at the major wax companies, especially Swix and Toko, and by the two companies that produce most of the sintered polyethylene for ski bases, Inter Montana Sport and Iso Sport. They were searching for ways to make downhill racing skis go fast enough to win World Cup races. Fortunately, they've also passed along to us a way to make our own skis turn better, glide better, and work better in any kind of snow.

As usual, I'm indebted to the editors of *SKI Magazine* for permission to adapt material that originally appeared in its pages.

Introduction:
Doing Quality Work

Every sport has its benchmark, the simple skill that separates the dilettantes from the aficionados. Rivermen used to spot a fellow fast-water expert by his J-stroke—if you had a J-stroke, you knew how to handle a canoe, and if you didn't, you'd be better off in front of an outboard motor on flatwater. A climber has either led, or he hasn't; top-roping doesn't count. Real drivers know how to double-clutch. Blue-water sailors know their celestial. And so on.

Some skiers may argue that the benchmark for us is possession of a carved turn, or experience in bottomless Utah powder, or an adventure down Corbett's Couloir, or a NASTAR gold medal. But I always look at a skier's bases.

You can tell a lot about the way a skier turns—and about his attitude toward skiing—by looking at his bases and edges. You can tell whether he spends too much time on his tails, whether he carves his turns, whether he skis with legs locked together or with good independent leg action, whether he stems, whether one of his legs is stronger than the other, or whether he swivels his turns in the bumps. Most of all, you can tell from the condition of his skis whether he is interested in improving, or is a terminal intermediate.

It may be unfair to say that a good skier—one who skis easily and aggressively in all kinds of terrain—is a terminal intermediate if he doesn't tune his skis regularly. But I've never met a skier with skills I respect who doesn't run a thumb over his edges once a day. Nor have I met a good skier who hasn't figured out a way to make his boots fit really well. If you're going to do high-quality work at anything, you need the right tools. Skis and boots are the skier's tools.

The fact is that you can't ski at the expert level with a marginal boot fit, concave bases, or rusty edges, any more than you can drive well with bald tires, loose steering, or gone-for-good shocks. This book will show you how to hone your skiing tools and thereby improve your skiing. But just as tuning your skis and boots right is the prerequisite to expert skiing, having the right tools and a proper workbench is the prerequisite to tuning skis properly.

Setting Up

You will need a solid workbench that is long enough to hold your skis, and you'll need a ski vise you can screw to it. An ordinary steel-jaw hardware store vise will certainly damage your bases and edges. Spend enough money to buy a good solid vise made of steel or cast aluminum that will screw firmly to the workbench, rather than a lightweight, extruded-alloy, clamp-on toy. This is one of the few items you won't find in even a good hardware store. Order a vise through your local ski shop or from a mail-order house specializing in ski-tuning supplies (see Appendix E at the end of this book for addresses).

You will need a new, sharp file—a 10-inch mill bastard file is best to start with. Get a wire brush or file card to keep the file in cutting condition. You'll need a high-quality steel cabinet scraper, a hard plastic scraper (acrylic works best), a sheet of plastic scrubbing pad, a pocket whetstone or piece of emery cloth, sandpaper in various fine grades, a brush with short nylon or brass bristles, a Stanley Sur-form file blade, some P-tex repair material, an assortment of ski waxes, a can of liquid wax remover, and a waxing iron. This is the basic kit—you can do any of the ski repairs in this book using only these tools, though from time to time I'll mention more specialized tools that can make certain jobs a bit easier.

You can save money on some tools. Most good ski shops sell prepackaged ski-tuning kits, with a basic assortment of these

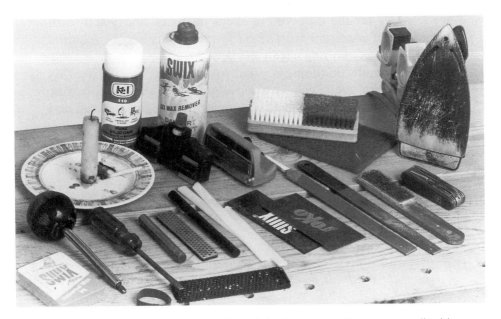

Basic ski-tuning kit includes (left to right from top) silicone spray, liquid wax remover, brass and nylon brush, Fibertex or Scotch-brite pad, ski vise, candle for lighting repair stick, edge-bevelling file, side-file holder, waxing iron, wax, Posidrive screwdriver, flat blade screwdriver, true bar, whetstone, polyethylene base repair material, plastic scraper, steel scraper, mill bastard files, file card, knife, Sur-form file, and rubber band for locking up ski brake.

tools—it's usually cheaper to buy the whole lot together than to buy the tools individually. Get an old clothing iron at a garage sale for $10. Files wear out: an inexpensive $3 carbon steel file from a hardware store may be good for 10 or 20 ski-tuning jobs, while a tough $8 chrome steel Swedish file from a ski shop may be good for 50 tunings. For your pocket whetstone, buy a $1 carborundum stone, a $4 Arkansas stone, or a $20 diamond stone.

Set up your workbench in a well-lighted, well-ventilated, well-heated area. You can't do good work in the dark, and a job done in a cold, drafty garage is bound to be done in a hurry and badly.

Ski tuning is a craft. It's very simple and straightforward, but it takes practice. As you get better at it, the job becomes easier and the results improve. Before working on your expensive new skis, practice on your old skis. Then go skiing on your old skis. They'll work better for the time you've spent on them, and you'll learn what kind of edge-tune works best for you. Once you've acquired the touch, you won't damage your new skis.

Like any craft, ski tuning is a skill you can take pride in. Working smoothly with good tools is a sensuous thing, and a ski in fine condition is among man's most elegant artifacts. Enjoy the craft and it will help you enjoy the sport more fully.

PART I
SKIS

1
When Skis Are New

When a ski arrives at a ski shop, carefully packaged in a plastic sleeve and a cardboard box, it's not yet ready for the snow. Obviously, it still needs bindings. Less obviously, it still needs a careful tune-up and waxing.

This is true of most skis, even those called "factory tuned," which are shipped with a coat of wax in place. The wax is there primarily to keep the edges from rusting in the long sea voyage from some European or Japanese port to a U.S. Customs shed. But all factory tuning jobs are done on high-speed machines, not by hand. And automatic machinery doesn't always do a very good job of tuning skis.

To understand why this is so you should first know something about the way skis are built. The component parts of a ski—its core, its fiberglass and aluminum structural layers, its steel edges and polyethylene running surface, its ABS plastic topskin and sidewalls, and its plastic or aluminum protective top edges—are all coated with strong phenolic or epoxy adhesives and assembled together in a precisely machined steel mold. This mold is then placed in a large hydraulic press, where the components are cooked at anywhere between 210 degrees and 300 degrees Fahrenheit, depending on the type of glue, and pressed at about 150 pounds per square inch. The

1

adhesive liquefies and is pressed into every tiny gap and pore in the structure. After 15 or 20 minutes the mold is allowed to cool, it is removed from the press, and the ski is pried out, still quite warm.

After the ski returns to room temperature, the finishing operations begin. All the molding flash and excess resin are ground off, the top and bottom are quickly sanded smooth, and the ski is sent to the silk-screening room for a brightly colored paint job.

The ski is now cool enough to handle, but it is not yet stable. The resins inside are still curing, even two days later. If you've ever worked with fiberglass to repair a boat or auto body, you know that the fast-cure resins are not the strongest ones. The strongest resins cure slowly, so that their molecules can cross-link thoroughly and completely. The bonds in skis have to be even stronger than the bonds in civil aircraft, so the epoxies used are generally of the slow-cure variety. The ski undergoes minor dimensional changes during this slow-cure period. Most ski factories can't afford to let skis stack up in a curing room while this process is completed. The final base grind is normally done before the ski is silk-screened.

Why New Skis Are Not Flat

The final base grind leaves the edges sharp and square and the base fairly flat, almost flat enough to ski on. Final dimensional variations as the ski finishes curing will put bulges or hollows in the base. It's not at all unusual for a new ski to arrive at the ski shop concave or convex or both.

In addition, the final base grind is done on automatic equipment—the ski is fed across the grinding wheels by a moving belt. Theoretically, power-fed operations should be smoother and more consistent than hand-fed work, but that's not the way it works out. Instead, powerfeed variations arising from worn belts, out-of-round drive wheels, current fluctuations, and so on frequently produce longitudinal waves in the finished base.

A fast coat of wax can cover some of these waves and bulges, but only until the skis touch the snow. If you want to be assured of skiing on a flat, smooth ski, a ski that runs and turns the way it was designed to, it's necessary to hand tune it first, filing it flat and ironing a coat of wax deep into the polyethylene base. Only hand filing or careful wet sanding on a specially designed platen tuning machine can make a ski flat enough for high-performance skiing.

Runout gauge shows this brand new ski .003 inch concave. A good skier would consider this ski notchy and unresponsive; an intermediate would find it very difficult to begin turns on this ski, but would most likely blame himself. The ski should be filed flat and then bevelled and waxed before anyone skis on it.

How Flat Is Flat?

A really flat ski is level across its width within about .002 inch—two one-thousandths of an inch. To measure this minute dimension would require the precision of a micrometer or a mechanic's run-out gauge. Most good skiers can, however, actually feel the difference between a flat ski and a ski that's concave by .005 inch. Racers can feel the difference at less than .001 inch. I've seen brand-new skis, fresh out of the factory wrapping, that are off by .01 inch or more.

While you would need sensitive instruments to measure this amount of deviation, you can see it. Place a ski in a vise, base up, and clean the factory wax off it with wax remover and a clean rag. You'd do this anyway—you won't want to ski on the factory's shipping wax. Hang a light source over the ski tip. I use an articulated, high-intensity desk lamp on the end of my workbench, but an ordinary auto shop trouble light would be just as good. Place a good straightedge, either a mechanic's true bar or the clean edge of a steel ski scraper, across the base and sight, or look, up into the light. Light should shine between the plastic base and the scraper in a smooth, even line across the ski. Bright spots show where the base is low, dark spots show where it's high.

Ski Base Profiles

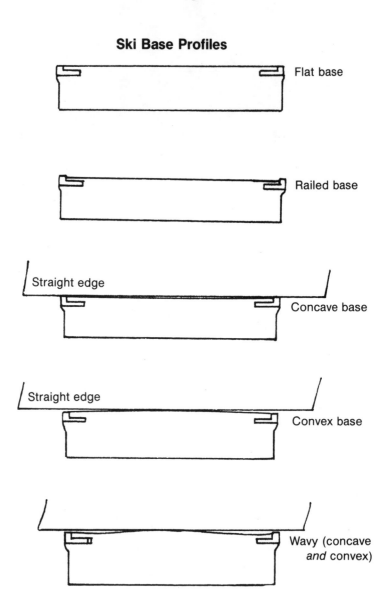

To judge a ski's flatness, place a straightedge or true bar across the base and sight under it, against a bright light. This ski is flat. Light shining over the edges indicates that it has been bevelled. This ski is well tuned and ready to ski. Be sure to check flatness at several points along the ski's length. You may find it flat in some spots, concave or convex at others.

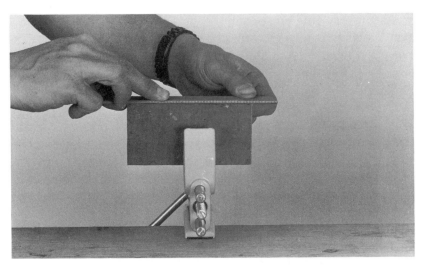

To create a good straightedge or to sharpen a steel scraper, lock the scraper in a vise and file the long edge straight, keeping the file flat.

Concave Bases

If the scraper rests squarely on the two steel edges and light appears under the scraper at the center of the ski sole, the ski is concave. If you ski on it, it will feel edgy and recalcitrant—it won't want to turn. It will want to run fast, in a straight line, and to turn you'll have to unweight very aggressively—you may actually have to jump and swivel the skis while they're off the snow. Concave skis are exhausting and frustrating, and can even be dangerous. It's easy to catch an uphill edge with concave skis. Half the trouble inexperienced skiers have with their equipment is due to bases that are worn concave. And there's the rub—because even the toughest plastics are softer than the steel edges, all skis eventually become concave simply from being skied on the abrasive snow. Periodically, you'll have to take the concavity out of any ski you use by flat-filing.

Flat-Filing

Make concave skis flat by filing the steel edges down level with the polyethylene sole. If the concavity is severe, you'll need a very aggressive file—use a 12-inch body file or a double-cut file. In extreme cases, ask your ski shop to run the skis over the wet-belt sander or stone grinder. Be aware that excessive pressure when stone grinding or power sanding bases can case harden the edges, making it very difficult to hand file them later. So rely on a ski shop that knows how to run its machines conservatively. Few new skis nowadays need this kind of treatment, though older, long-neglected skis frequently do.

Once the base has been taken down to a fairly flat rough finish, you're ready to flat-file. Inspect your new skis. If they have one-piece continuous edges, you may file from either end—from tip to tail or tail to tip. If they have cracked or segmented edges, made with hairline fissures every inch or so, you can file only tip to tail, or else you'll file deeper gaps into the fissures. You'll find cracked edges most often on slalom racing skis, on some softer recreational and mogul skis, and on powder skis.

The standard tool for flat-filing is an 8- or 10-inch mill bastard file; the 10-inch size is stiffer and therefore easier to use when learning—you're less likely to bend it, thereby filing the ski convex. Since the teeth of most files are oriented at about a 30-degree angle

Before working on the base and edges, lock up the ski brake with a thick rubber band . . .

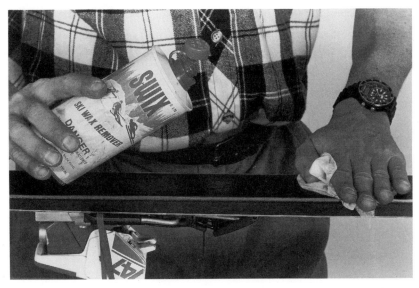

. . . and clean the old wax off the base with a liquid wax remover. If you leave old wax on the base, it will clog up the teeth of your files and gum up your whetstone.

across the width of the file body, to put the teeth at an efficient cutting angle to the ski base, the file should be held at about a 45-degree angle to the ski's length. You'll occasionally see special "long-angle" files with teeth cut at about 60 degrees, and these files can be held directly across the ski.

All files cut in one direction only. If you are going to push the file along, hold the tang—the sharp narrow end—in your right hand and the off end or square end in your left hand. With the ski firmly clamped base up in the vise, place the file flat on the ski base, with a thumb placed over each edge of the ski on top of the file to put pressure right on the edges. Pressing down farther out may bend the file, giving you a convex base.

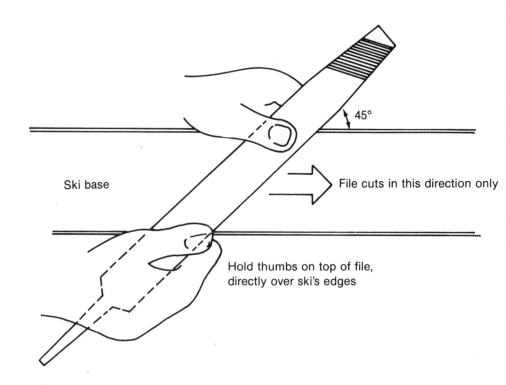

45°

Ski base

File cuts in this direction only

Hold thumbs on top of file, directly over ski's edges

Flat-file the base by pushing the file in long, even strokes. Thumbs are placed over the ski edges to prevent bending the file. The tang is in the right hand, the off end in the left, and the file is pushed in the cutting direction. Don't drag the file back; lift it between strokes.

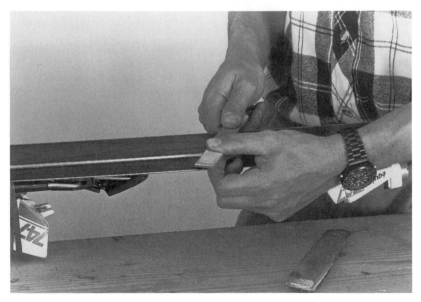

Another view of the flat-file position.

Now push the file along, holding it at that 45-degree angle, and feel it cut the steel edges. Use moderate pressure—if the file is new and sharp, you can actually see the steel filings curling off the edges. Use a rag to clean these filings off the base frequently, so they won't be driven into the plastic.

After several strokes of the file, clean off the tiny metal shavings so they won't be driven into the plastic base . . .

Push the file in long, smooth strokes. If it feels like it's catching and skipping, hold the file at a slightly different angle or alter the pressure—skipping means that you will wind up with a slightly scalloped and very unpredictable edge.

As you work, keep the file and ski base clean. After every third or fourth stroke, clean the file vigorously with your file card; turn the file over after every stroke to use the clean teeth on the other side.

Some people feel more comfortable pulling the file instead of pushing it. If you want to do it that way, hold the tang in your left hand and the off end in your right, find the right 45-degree angle to get an efficient cut, and pull away.

... and clean the file with vigorous strokes of the file card.

Convex Bases

If, when you inspect the base with your straightedge, it rocks from edge to edge on a fulcrum near the middle of the sole, then the ski is convex. The ski will swivel sometimes when you want it to track accurately. When you're trying to run straight it may wander right and left and may try to cross over the other ski's tip. It won't bite very aggressively on hard snow and will usually feel very unpredictable. You must flatten it by removing enough plastic to make the sole level with the edges.

You can sometimes do this with a sharp steel scraper. Use a brand-new scraper or file a clean, straight sharp edge in an old scraper by clamping it in a vise and filing lengthwise along the edge. Holding the scraper firmly in both hands and being careful not to bend it, scrape the length of the ski. The excess polyethylene should come off smoothly in thin sheets and curls. If the scraper skips or catches, it isn't sharp enough or you're holding it at the wrong angle or pressing too hard. Be smooth. You don't want to scrape steps into the base.

A safer way to bring a convex base down flat is to file it—you run little risk of bending a file far enough to make the ski concave. Stop often as you flat-file to clean the accumulating plastic from the file teeth.

In any filing operation, draw the file only in its cutting direction. Don't drag it back along the ski base in the no-cut direction. That only dulls the teeth of the file (the teeth can't be resharpened) and drives shavings into the plastic base. Check your progress every few minutes by sighting under the straightedge and stop filing when the ski looks flat. No sense in wasting time and elbow grease, not to mention base material.

It's important to check your progress at several points along the ski's length. I've seen skis that were convex in the shovel and tail but concave in the middle. You want to be sure that the ski is flat along its full length.

This is the toughest job you'll ever have to do on your skis. Once made flat, a daily or weekly touch-up with the file will prevent them from becoming as concave or convex again. When both skis are flat and smooth, clean your file, and then get ready for a quick edge-filing.

Edge-Filing

Edges should be sharp enough to shave a thin curl off the flat of a fingernail. New skis usually don't need much in the way of edge-filing—the flat-filing operation normally takes enough metal off to leave a sharp, clean edge. A quick once-over will clean up any bad burrs left over from the previous filing, or from a power grinding operation. Edge-filing, sometimes called *side-filing*, is tricky. You have to run the file along the edge in the cutting direction (tang trailing) while holding the file at a consistent right angle to the flat base. This can be done, with practice, by hand, but it's easier to use a file holder designed for the purpose.

File holders are easy to get at most ski shops. Make sure the one you get fits your file. I'm not impressed with most commercially available edge files. These are usually small pocket-size devices meant for use on the hill. The file blades supplied with them are rarely very good. They're either too small, with an inefficient crosshatch pattern, or too aggressive, with the big razorlike teeth of a body file, able to take off huge metal shavings in one stroke. Your best bet for edge-filing is an ordinary 8-inch mill bastard file, with an appropriate file holder.

Any time a file cuts the steel edge, it leaves a thin sharp edge of deformed steel overhanging the adjoining surface. This edge is

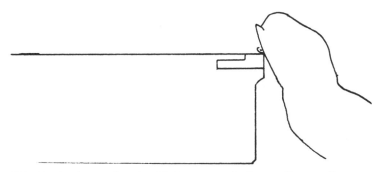

Ski edge is sharp when it will shave a curl off your fingernail

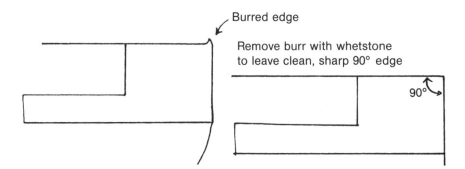

Burred edge

Remove burr with whetstone
to leave clean, sharp 90° edge

90°

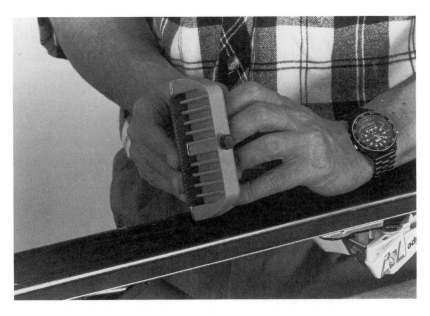

A file holder makes it easy to file the edge at a 90-degree angle.

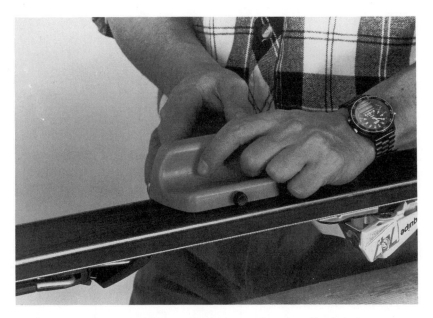

The teeth in the file holder cut in only one direction. Push in long, overlapping strokes, and don't drag the file backward.

called the *burr*, though it's different from the burr left by impact on a rock. You can minimize the burr left from edge-filing by inserting the file in its holder in such a way that the file teeth, as they angle along the edge, turn the burr to the top of the edge rather than to the base of the edge. It makes sense if you think of the angled file teeth as the blades of a snowplow—visualize the direction in which those blades will move the steel as they cut, and make sure they move the steel away from the ski's running surface. This means that you'll edge-file from tip to tail down one edge, and from tail to tip down the other. As with flat-filing, work in long, smooth, overlapping strokes, and clean the base, file, and file holder guide surface—the surface that rests against the ski base—frequently.

If you want to try edge-filing without a file holder (most experienced tuners don't bother with holders), lock the ski in the vise vertically, with the base facing away from you, edge up. Hold the file against the edge with your hand curled over and your knuckles resting on the ski base, as a guide. File in long, smooth strokes, pressing lightly. Clean the file frequently and brush the shavings off the sidewall and base.

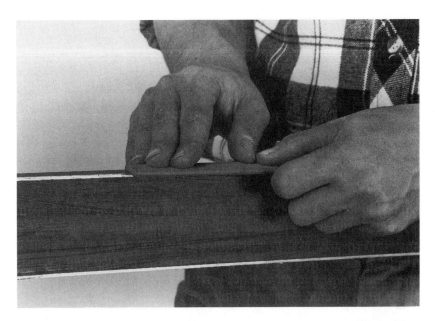

Expert ski tuners use a mill bastard file on the edge, holding it at a 90-degree angle by bracing the knuckles of the left hand against the base.

You may find that even a new file slides over the edge without cutting—it's almost as if the file were bouncing off the edge. If so, the steel edge has probably been case-hardened. Case-hardened steel has been heat-treated to make the surface very hard, leaving the interior of the metal softer and more resilient; in effect, the mild steel is given a tough casing. It's a common process for lock shackles and chain links, but ski edges are not supposed to be case hardened; they're supposed to be of a uniform hardness, slightly softer than a carbon steel file.

Edges get case-hardened when a grinding or sanding machine develops too much friction heat, tempering the steel. An inexperienced or careless operator can case harden your steel edges easily by applying too much pressure to the ski as it goes over a stone grinder. This is a fairly common occurrence in the ski-shop preparation of new skis. Fortunately, it's easy to fix. All you need is a pocket whetstone.

Use the whetstone the same way you use the mill bastard file. Draw it in long overlapping strokes along both surfaces of each edge, pressing vigorously this time to work through the case-hardened surface. After a few strokes of the whetstone, the steel file should cut into the edge. You may find this operation necessary even before you flat-file a new ski.

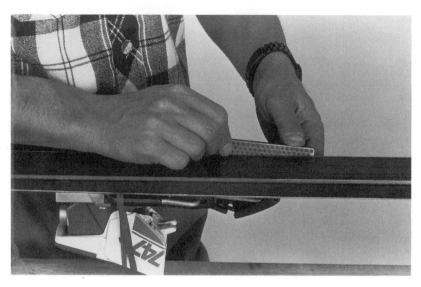

When the edge has been case hardened or burred, clean it up with a whetstone on the side edge . . .

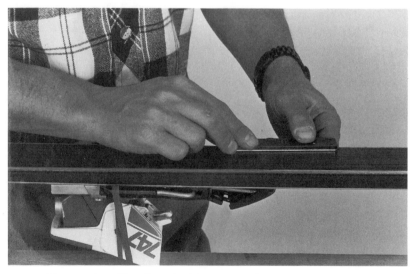

. . . and base edge. Use the whetstone exactly as you'd use a file, but remember that the whetstone produces a finer, more polished finish.

Use the whetstone exactly the same way after edge-filing to remove the burr from the edge of the base; there may be a microscopic burr there even if you oriented the file to move steel in the other direction. A burred edge looks and feels sharp—it may even cut the skin. On snow, a burred edge feels like a concave ski—edgy, catchy, and unpredictable.

Finally, use the whetstone to detune the edge at tip and tail—deburr the edges vigorously here, holding the stone at a 45-degree angle to the corner of the edge—to reduce the ski's tendency to hook. Don't round the edge—if we wanted a round edge, we'd use a file for this operation.

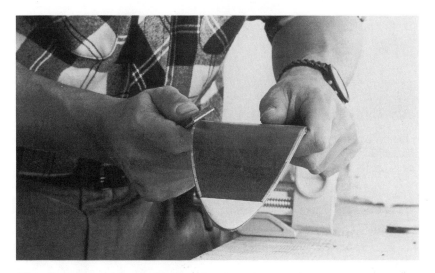

The whetstone is the tool to use for detuning the tip and tail. Moderate pressure and a 45-degree angle produce a deburred finish without seriously rounding the steel edge.

The whetstone is the most important tool you have. Use it to prepare a case-hardened edge for filing, to deburr the edge after filing, and to detune the tip and tail.

The last filing operation knocks the sharp edge off the aluminum tip and tail protectors. This is important. In wet snow and on moguls, sharp edges and corners at the ski's extremities can hang up and spill you. Clamp the ski with its base up and file all the edges of the tail bar to smooth, round surfaces, using a mill bastard file. Do the same for the tip protector—it's just a safety measure.

Use an old file to round off the corners and edges of the aluminum tail bar. The same file can serve to remove aluminum splinters from the ski's protective top edge and tip protector.

As always, finish the filing by cleaning up all metal and plastic shavings. Now it's time to wax your skis.

Hot Wax

All ski waxes are applied to the ski's base, but the concept of the *base wax* means something else. The base wax is the "median" or soft base-sealing wax, a moderate-temperature wax applied as a first coat to a brand-new ski base. Refer to the wax manufacturer's color chart and choose as a base wax the color that lies just on the cold side of freezing (see Appendix C). For example, Toko Red and Swix Violet make good base waxes. If you don't have the proper base wax, no matter—any wax is better than no wax, for the same reason that any oil is better than no oil when your car engine is down a quart.

Very simply, wax seals the base and protects it against oxidation. We tend to think of most plastics, including polyethylene, as impervious to the elements, nonbiodegradable, and indestructable. But polyethylene does oxidize, and ultraviolet light speeds the oxidation process greatly. There's a lot of UV light flying around on a bright winter day, especially at high elevations. It burns your eyes and nose, and it breaks down the long, tough molecules in polyethylene so they'll combine with free oxygen in the atmosphere. When that happens, the plastic begins to turn milky in color, and it loses its ability to bead or repel water. The base becomes sticky and sluggish. You can stop the process simply by keeping a sealer coat of wax on your skis, to bar oxygen from penetrating the plastic. And wax glides more smoothly than even brand-new unoxidized polyethylene.

Set your iron's thermostat for *wool*. Melt the end of the bar of wax on the sole of the iron, with the iron's tip held a few inches above the ski's base—don't touch the hot metal directly to the bare, unwaxed base. Drip a long bead of wax down the length of the ski on one side of the center groove, then up the other side (a lot of modern skis have no center groove; just make a zigzag or sine wave bead). Set the wax aside and iron the bead into the base thoroughly. Keep the iron moving so you won't burn the wax, but iron continuously for several minutes to melt it deep into the base.

Drip the wax onto the ski by melting a bar of wax against the iron. Don't touch the hot iron to the bare base.

Use enough wax so the iron will "float" on the liquid wax as you iron it into the base. If the wax smokes, the iron is too hot. Keep the wax liquid, and keep the iron moving.

After the wax has cooled to room temperature (at least 20 minutes), scrape it down smooth with a plastic scraper. Hold the scraper flat and straight. The plastic scraper is hard enough to cut into the polyethylene base if you bend or cup it.

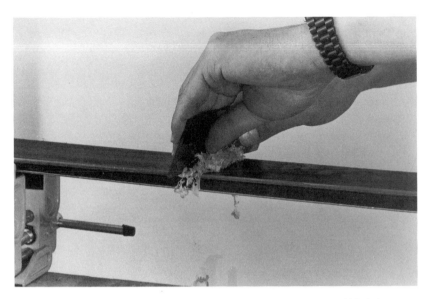

Another view of the plastic scraper drawing the wax down. Work in long, overlapping strokes. The object is to leave only a microscopic film of wax on the base.

Clean out the base groove with a dull screwdriver, with the end of a spoon, or with the corner of a specially shaped scraper.

Keep your plastic scraper straight and sharp by filing it flat
occasionally. This scraper is of acrylic (Plexiglas), a hard, tough plastic.

Don't worry about damaging the ski. Remember that it was
molded well above the boiling temperature of water, and that
melted wax isn't even hot enough to burn your skin much. Many
skis—most metal skis, for instance—will bend over backward as you
iron, acquiring an interesting reverse camber, as their bottom layers
expand with the heat. Don't worry about it. As long as the wax
doesn't smoke, the base isn't too hot. Just keep the iron moving, and
keep the wax on the surface liquid.

After a few minutes, when the wax is thoroughly worked in, let
the ski cool until the wax looks dry along the entire length of the ski.
Then take it out of the vise and wax the other ski. You can leave the
thick coat of wax on the ski to protect the base and edges for
travel—racers call this thick coat their "road wax"—or, if you plan
to ski soon, let the skis cool to room temperature, then scrape them
down smooth with your plastic scraper. Don't forget to clean out
the base groove with a dull screwdriver.

Clean up your workbench and get a beer. It's almost guaranteed
to snow tonight.

2
Keeping at It

Now that your skis are flat, sharp, and sealed—better than new—you will find that discipline keeps them that way with minimum effort. By discipline I mean the simple determination to find ten minutes each week to touch up your skis. Running the file lightly over your skis after two days of skiing will keep them flat. If, on the other hand, you let your tuning go for weeks at a time, when you finally get around to it you'll find your skis very concave again.

If you ski every weekend, the best time to tune your skis is as soon as you get home. That way you can clean all the road grime off your bases and bindings before they start corroding. Most skiers I know are exhausted on Sunday night, and they have a tendency to leave the skis standing in the closet until the following weekend. If your skis travel on top of the car, a ski bag will save you the trouble of having to clean them as soon as you get home. Open the bag when you arrive so the skis will dry out thoroughly. Then you can pull the skis out Thursday night and tune them while you watch the weekend weather report.

Tuning skis regularly is especially important for high-performance skis with sintered bases (see Chapter 4). Because of the way they are made, sintered bases are more porous than ordinary extruded bases. They hold wax better, but when they dry out air gets into the pores so they tend to oxidize and degrade faster. It's important to keep sintered bases waxed all the time. Remember our engine oil analogy—if you have an expensive Porsche, you change the oil more often than you do if you have a Chevy station wagon.

As you settle down for your weekly ski-tuning session, check first for rock-damaged edges. Just run a finger lightly up and down each steel edge. The rough spots are where you glanced off boulders. Most of these rough spots will be slightly case hardened by the heat generated from the impact. A file will probably only bounce off the rock burrs. Use your whetstone first to smooth out the rock burrs before you flat-file and edge-file.

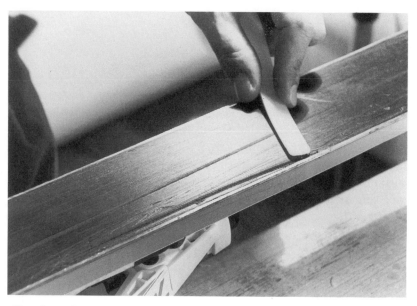

Classic springtime rock damage includes deep gouges in the base and rock burrs on the edges. The burrs are case hardened and need to be polished down with a whetstone before the edge can be filed. The white stick is P-tex repair material.

Rock burrs are often accompanied by small gouges in the polyethylene base. See Chapter 5 on how to repair these gouges. The time to repair a base gouge is before you flat-file the ski.

Remember to clean the old wax off the ski base with wax remover and a rag before flat-filing. After edge-filing and deburring, get out the iron and melt in a new coat of wax. Turn the ski over and check the binding for loose screws and damaged parts (see Chapter 13). Put the skis back in their bag and pack your duds.

I can't overemphasize the importance of doing this drill regularly. Pros do it daily, as do good instructors. Racers, of course, tune and wax every night. If you do it daily, it takes no more than ten minutes. But if you do it twice each season, it takes an hour. Both you and your edges will be rusty.

The most time-consuming part of the maintenance drill is patching the base gouges. If you do it daily, you'll have only one or two small dings to do each day, except in the late spring. One small ding is a quick, no-fuss repair. But repairing a dozen wounds on each ski, the harvest of weeks of neglect, is a major task.

3
Performance Tuning

Just as you can change a car's handling by changing its springs, shocks, and tire pressures, you can make a ski behave almost any way you'd like by changing the sharpness and bevel of its edges and base. This chapter concerns ski handling—making a ski turn more smoothly and easily in various snow conditions.

Detuning Skis

There is more to performance tuning than making a ski flat and picking the right wax. You can actually make a ski behave "stiffer" or "softer" by filing and sharpening it appropriately. A little handiwork with a file can turn a recalcitrant, straight-running missile into an easy-turning pussycat. Long skis are stable in part because they grip well at the ends, where they have the most leverage over your legs. If you reduce the ski's grip at shovel and tail, it will behave like a softer, or more maneuverable, ski. It will swivel more easily on moguls and in heavy or crusted snow. Then, by gradually restoring edge bite at the extremities, you can regain the ski's higher performance level. This dull 'em and tune 'em process can help an intermediate skier learn to handle a longer, stiffer ski, or it can be used to detune a hard-snow ski for soft-snow conditions. Conversely, it's also possible to over-sharpen a soft ski, giving it the grip on ice its designer never meant it to provide.

There are two ways to detune skis. You can simply dull the edges at tip and tail, or you can file a bevel into the edges. In recent years most ski factories have come to recommend edge-bevelling, and many good skis are bevelled as part of the final base grind before leaving the factory.

It's easy to dull the tip and tail whenever you need to—just carry a pocket whetstone or a piece of emery cloth when you go skiing. Make your first run of the morning on your freshly tuned skis, and feel them out. The skis may feel easy to turn, stable, smooth, and predictable, in which case you're all set. But on freshly sharpened edges, the skis may feel abrupt, hooky, nervous, and unpredictable. If that's the case, you'll want to dull back the tip and tail a bit with your whetstone.

Dull the edges back two inches at a time, starting at the widest part of the shovel and tail and working inward toward the middle. After a couple tries you'll find the level of tune where the ski feels comfortably quick. Don't use a file for edge-dulling. A file is far too aggressive a blade, and you can easily overdo it, dulling the edge permanently. You only want to round the edge very slightly, enough to feel the difference in turning, but not so much that you can't restore a sharp corner with just a few gentle strokes of the file.

How far back to dull the edges depends on how "short" you want the ski to behave. A six-inch dull-back is about the limit. Experiment: dull the tip and tail two inches, then go skiing; if the ski still feels long and awkward, dull the edges an additional two inches, and so on.

It is possible to overdo the edge-dulling. Experienced ski tuners do it all the time on demo skis they lend out in ski shops. I picked up a pair of brand-new Dynastar giant slalom skis at a shop in Sun Valley one day, expecting great things. But up on Warm Springs, the skis were just plain bad. A 207 cm giant slalom ski should be stable and should cut into the snow smoothly, progressively, and predictably when you roll it up on edge. This ski, fresh off the truck from the factory and carefully hand tuned, wandered around sideways and, when edged, grabbed and skipped. When I checked the skis with a true bar I found they were flat—so that wasn't the problem. The problem was that the tuner had dulled the edges back too aggressively.

This happens a lot. When ski shops send out long skis they don't often believe that the customer wants a 208 or a 204. So they dull the edges back to make the ski behave like a 195. With their edges round at the shovel, the skis won't bite. They wash out and kick instead.

That night I ran the 207s over a wet sander in the back of another ski shop and made sure the edges were square and sharp to the ends. The next morning they behaved just right: smooth, stable, solid. Great skis.

The lesson is that you can ruin a good pair of skis with unnecessary dulling. Edge-dulling should be done on the hill, using a pocket stone. It should be done only as necessary to make the skis comfortable, and no more.

Bevelling

The other technique for detuning skis is to bevel the edges with a file. The bevel is subtle, no more than one or two one-hundredths of an inch, equivalent to a one- or two-degree angle. That's enough to keep skis from hooking and to permit a smooth, rolling entry into the turn with no sacrifice in edging or carving ability.

The simplest bevelling tool is a mill bastard file with a length of duct tape around the tang end. The bevelling stroke is the same as the flat-filing stroke, but the thickness of the tape puts a slight bevel on the opposite edge.

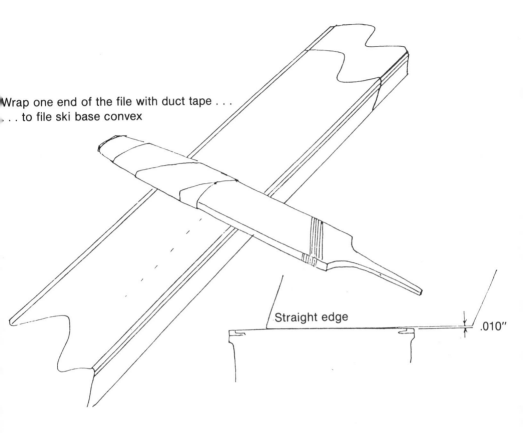

Wrap one end of the file with duct tape . . .
. . . to file ski base convex

Straight edge

.010″

Skis with durable sintered bases can be bevelled when new, then left untouched through several ski-tuning cycles. Restore the bevel after half a dozen hand tunings, or after any pass over a stone grinder or wet-belt sander.

The simplest tool for bevelling is a mill bastard file with a length of tape around the off end. The tape holds the file at a shallow angle to the base as you file. Flat-file the ski first, then tape the file and make six or eight passes up each edge.

Different skis demand different degrees of edge bevel. Some companies—Dynamic, Volkl, and Olin, for example—say their skis should not be bevelled at all. K2 recommends a one-degree bevel, and some ski tuners put as much as a two-degree bevel in certain Rossignol models. In general, torsionally stiff skis need a deeper bevel angle than torsionally soft skis.

Torsional stiffness depends primarily on ski construction. Aluminum sandwich skis with foam cores—skis like the Rossignol SM and 3G—are very stiff torsionally, and need the deepest bevel. Aluminum skis with wood cores, and torsion box skis, are moderate in torsion, and generally need a one-degree bevel. Fiberglass sandwich skis are usually soft in torsion, and need little or no bevel. Here's a chart of some popular ski models with some pointers on how to tune them.

You can tape a file differentially to give a one-degree bevel on one side and a two-degree bevel on the other—just lay more tape on one side of the file. In general, two layers of duct tape generate a one-degree bevel, four layers a two-degree bevel. Several manufacturers—Toko, Swix, and SKS, for instance—make adjustable bevelling tools you can set to produce any degree of bevel from zero to three degrees. Most of these tools can also be set to provide an equivalent variation in side bevel.

Some ski makers, notably Fischer, Blizzard, and Head, recommend filing a slightly acute angle into the edge of their slalom skis and even some GS (giant slalom) models. The adjustable bevelling tools are handy for this.

For a more precise bevel, use an adjustable bevelling file. This one, from Toko, adjusts for 0 to 3 degrees of bevel and 0 to 2 degrees of side-edge angle.

Edge-Tuning Chart

Ski Type	Typical Torsional Stiffness	Bevel
Foam-core metal laminates: Rossignol SM and 3g series, Dynastar MV5 and Acryglass series	1.9–2.5 Nm/degree	One degree under foot, feathering to 2 degrees at tip and tail
Wood-core metal laminates: Most Austrian, Italian, and Japanese giant slalom racing skis, plus many Austrian slalom skis; Fischer, Kastle, Atomic, Head, Kneissl, Blizzard, Spalding, Nishizawa, Kazama	1.2–1.8 Nm/degree	One degree full length; slalom skis may be flat under foot, feathering to 1 degree at tip and tail
Torsion box (wet wrap) skis: Most K2 and Volkl skis, some Rossignol, Pre and Blizzard slalom models; Fischer Vacuum Technic and Yamaha; Paramount fiberglass laminates	1.2–1.8 Nm/degree	One degree full length
Most fiberglass laminates: Most Olin and Elan Models, some Pre and RD racing skis; softer recreational skis from most manufacturers	.7–1.3 Nm/degree	Flat file; no bevel

Note: Dynamic and Volkl recommend that their torsion box and laminated skis be tuned flat, with no bevel.

The key to ski-tracking accuracy is that sharp ends bite and dull ends slide. Bearing this in mind, adjust your bevel and edge-dulling procedures to cure tricky ski problems. Are your tails so stiff that the skis seem to rudder or arrow straight ahead? Put more bevel in the tail, or dull the edges there further back, to balance the ski. Does your ski wash out when you try to initiate a quick, abrupt turn on very hard snow? Oversharpen the shovel, putting an acute angle into the edge instead of the normal 90-degree angle. Skis you want flat and sharp for hard snow can be bevelled for softer snow. Many race tuners leave the inside edges flat and sharp, bevelling or dulling the outside edges; if you try this, remember to mark your left and right skis clearly. Fifteen minutes of experimentation each morning, along with some handiwork with your pocket stone, can give you the skis you need for the day.

4
Speed Tuning

Waxing theory is pretty simple. Snow is composed of hard-edged crystals and is quite abrasive. If you've ever fallen while skiing fast in the spring, the snow may have taken some skin off your bare arm. The stuff feels just like sandpaper.

The ski doesn't glide directly on the sharp points and angles of the snow crystals. It glides instead on a microscopic film of water created as the ski presses against those sharp points. The same thing happens when you press an ice cube against the side of a glass—pressure creates heat, which melts the ice to conform to the glass. The meltwater lubricates the interface between ice and glass.

The ski slides best when this film of water takes the form of tiny individual droplets, which act like ball bearings under the base. If too much snow melts and forms a continuous sheet of water under the base, the suction created by the exclusion of air will slow down the glide. This happens often in wet spring snow. Water is 100 times more viscous than air, so the more air that can be kept in the mix under the base, the faster the ski will glide. In years past Austrian ski factories experimented with all kinds of ducting systems to force air under the ski, including big air scoops attached to the top of the ski and connected to air passages underneath.

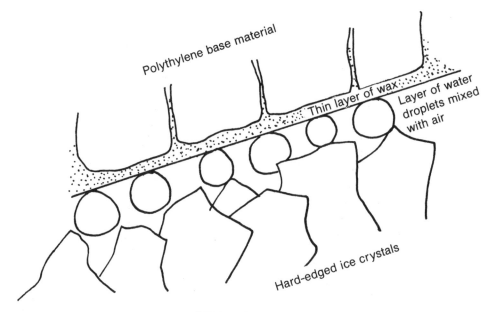

Gliding Mechanics

Water "sheets" on the unwaxed ski at the left, while it beads on the waxed ski on the right. When water sticks to a base, the result is suction, slow glide, and reluctance to turn. The smaller the water beads, the more air comes into the mix, and the faster the ski glides.

Polyethylene is a low-friction material with excellent strength, but it is highly wettable—that is, water sticks to it. If you pour water on an unwaxed ski base, the water sheets up instead of beading into the "ball bearings" you want to ski on. Moreover, polyethylene is slightly water absorbent. It's just porous enough to soak up and retain some moisture (have you ever tried to drink from a polyethylene water jar that once contained lemonade? The lemon taste never quite goes away). In order to create a nonwetting, nonabsorptive surface, you must seal the polyethylene with wax.

Wax Chemistry

One of the things that makes polyethylene an ideal ski base material is that it is a close chemical relative of paraffin. Paraffin molecules are very similar in size and composition to the basic ethyl units that link up in astoundingly long chains to make polyethylene, so the paraffin molecules have a good affinity to polyethylene. They fit very neatly into the intermolecular pores in the ski base, and they like to stay there. Paraffin seals the pores well and makes the ski nonabsorptive. A petroleum by-product, paraffin is also oily and therefore nonwetting. Water beads up and rolls right off it. So far it looks like an ideal ski wax.

Unfortunately, paraffin is also very soft. This means that the hard, sharp points and edges of snow and ice crystals dig into its soft surface, a process which can prevent a ski from sliding at all. When the snow is very cold, and you have soft wax on your skis, the snow tends to clump and stick on the bases, and you go nowhere. In order to harden the paraffin, wax manufacturers add various plasticizers, or hardeners, most of them chemical intermediaries between the paraffin and polyethylene molecules. The more plasticizers, the harder the wax. But the more plasticizers, the more wettable the material.

Very warm snow is high in water content and is composed of big, soft, rounded crystals. You can use a fairly soft wax, since the edges of the crystals aren't too sharp, but you need a nonwetting wax, because the snow is very wet. So "warm" waxes, those formulated for warm and wet snow, are largely paraffin, with a relatively small plasticizer content. Very cold fresh snow, on the other hand, contains little moisture and has very small, hard, sharply pointed crystals. Your ski base will need a much harder wax, but can have a more wettable surface, since the snow is largely air anyway (cold, new snow in Colorado, for instance, is generally only 6 to 8 percent moisture; in the Sierra, 8 to 12 percent). So "cold" waxes are heavy with plasticizers and somewhat farther along the continuum. Your job each morning is to judge the water content of the snow and the sharpness of the snow crystals and to select a wax with just the right level of hardness and wettability. Bear in mind that as snow lies on the ground it changes, gradually compacting down into rounder, wetter granules.

Color Codes

The wax manufacturers make it easy to select the proper wax by publishing very detailed waxing tables and color-coding waxes for temperature ranges. In general, "warm" colors—yellow, orange, and red—are for warm or wet snow, and "cool" colors—blue, violet, and green—for cold or dry snow. Study the table that comes with your wax assortment and follow the directions carefully. If you're worried about misjudging the wax, you're better off choosing a slightly harder wax than picking one that is too soft, and you're better off with a slightly wetted wax than one that the snow may clot on.

The major European wax makers use a soft-base wax that melts at about 139°F. They then add harder waxes to get the right blend for each temperature range. The American companies Slick and Hertel use plasticizers as hardening agents. Hertel also adds a wetting agent that helps water bead in spite of the fairly low wettability of its hard-base wax. Many race-prep technicians broaden the temperature ranges of their standard waxes by mixing in some Hertel wax.

Waxes may always be blended to handle intermediate temperatures. In fact, most wax manufacturers recommend blending and provide blending formulas on their waxing tables. Blending waxes is easy when you are ironing the wax in. If the chart calls for one part red and two parts blue, for instance, just hold one bar of red wax sandwiched between two bars of blue and press the end of the sandwich against the iron to drip the purple mix on the ski base. Then iron the mixed wax as usual. Needing to know which waxes to blend and when to blend them is one good reason to stick with a single brand of wax and learn its color-coding well.

Textured Wax

Come spring, when the snow is wet and slushy, or "corned up," a good tactic is to use a reasonably hard base wax and carry a bar of softer wax in a small plastic bag, along with your pocket stone. If too much wettability is making your skis sluggish, crayon the warm wax over the hard wax and leave it fairly rough. You can mark a series of Xs along the length of the ski with the wax—the rough texture of the wax will help break up the surface tension. It's easy to apply a soft wax over a hard one and impossible to apply a hard wax over a soft one. This is another reason to wax a bit on the hard side.

Ski waxes generally melt between about 120° and 170° Fahrenheit. The harder the wax, the higher the melting temperature. Polyethylene itself melts at about 850° Fahrenheit, but the plastic base may delaminate if you melt the glue that holds it on, and that can happen above about 300° Fahrenheit.

The hard waxes should be ironed-in thoroughly and scraped smooth. In very warm snow, a traditional practice is to apply a thick coat of soft wax by painting it on. Melt a bar of wax in a small saucepan over a low flame. Don't overcook it or the wax will burn— if it starts to smoke, remove it from the stove immediately. Use a natural bristle paintbrush just wider than the ski base. Nylon bristles are a poor choice because nylon itself has a low melting temperature and may actually melt in the hot wax. Paint the wax on in long strokes, starting at the tail and moving forward. The step formed at the beginning of each stroke will help break up the surface tension. Clean out the base groove, too. This will introduce an air channel that may reduce the suction in very wet snow.

Base Structure

The discovery that the base groove affects suction led to the discovery that a ski will run faster if the base is structured, or textured. A structured base is one with thousands of tiny grooves sanded into the polyethylene, all running lengthwise along the ski. The grooves channel off meltwater and bring more air into the mix, mechanically producing ball-bearing water beads. For ultimate speed on the race course, skis should be structured. Proper base preparation and choice of wax together can be worth at least a one-second improvement on a typical 30-second NASTAR course.

To structure a base, first remove all the old wax with liquid wax remover, do any base repair necessary, and sand the base down flat. Use a sanding block, or wrap a sheet of sandpaper around a stiff flat file. Use a good quality silicon carbide sandpaper, and choose the grit according to snow conditions (see Appendix D for the appropriate structure size). In general, cold snow requires a finer groove structure, wet snow a coarser pattern.

An easy way to structure the base is to sand it with 180 grit silicon carbide paper. Use a sanding block or wrap the sandpaper around your file. As usual, be careful not to bend the file. Sand in long, even strokes along the ski's length.

Sand the ski base in long, overlapping strokes, beginning at the tip. Two or three passes should be sufficient, unless the skis are new and still have longitudinal waves in the base left over from a power grind. If you can see waves by sighting down the length of the ski, sand the waves out. It may require firm pressure and several changes of sandpaper.

After sanding, brush out the structure with a brass bristle brush (if you don't have a brass brush, use one with stiff nylon bristles). Brush only longitudinally, tip to tail; the purpose of brushing is to clean any silicon carbide particles out of the grooves in the

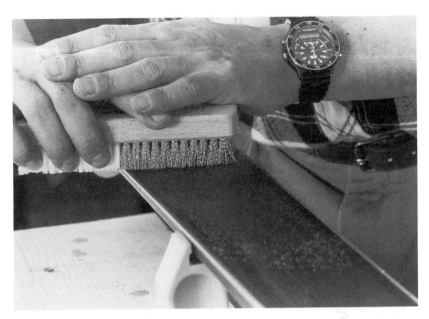

Use a brass brush to clean out the sanded structure. Brush along the grooves.

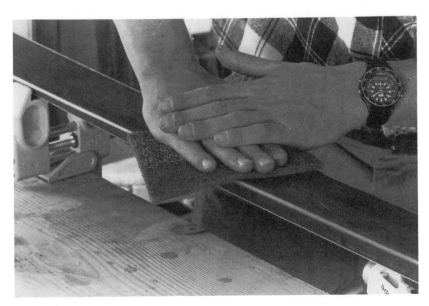

Follow up the structuring process by polishing along the ski's length, in long strokes, with the Fibertex or Scotch-brite pad. This scrubbing action orients any loose fibers along the structure grooves.

structure, along with loose strands of polyethylene, and to orient all the remaining plastic particles with the grooves. Finish the base by polishing it with a plastic scrubbing pad—use a 3M Scotch-brite pad from the grocery store or a Swix Fibertex pad. Once again, polish only in one direction, tip to tail, so the whole base structure lines up parallel.

Now iron-in a coat of warm base wax and scrape it off with a plastic scraper while still warm. This lifts out any remaining foreign particles. Brush and scrub the base once more and iron-in your race wax according to the expected snow conditions. Let the skis cool for at least 20 minutes at room temperature, then scrape them smooth with a plastic scraper.

Finally, to open up the base structure, brush the scraped surface with your nylon brush. This will produce a waxy powder on the ski surface, consisting of tiny balls of wax brushed out of the grooves. Lightly brush this powder away, then scrape and brush the base again. Don't polish the base. That will simply flatten out the structure.

Once you've structured a good sintered polyethylene base, the hard plastic will hold the pattern for most of the season. The only reason to repeat the hand-sanding process is to repair the structure if the skis have sustained rock damage or after a power grinding, or if you are preparing the skis to race in radically different snow conditions that require a different structure. But each time you wax the structured skis for a race, you'll need to brush the final scraped wax out of the structure grooves.

At very high speeds—50 mph and up—the waxing rules change. At speeds this high, friction between ski and snow creates enough heat to increase the amount of moisture under the ski dramatically. The ski tends to plane on that moisture, which doesn't have time to pass through a fine sanded structure. So for downhill racing and speed trials, technicians choose softer waxes to compensate for the additional water, and often use a more open structure to channel the water off faster.

Recreational Waxes

If you don't intend to race, some of the newer broad-spectrum waxes can save you the trouble of picking and blending a wax. Hertel Hot Sauce, mentioned above, is a good example. Most wax companies also offer special waxes designed to be rubbed on or applied directly from a can, in liquid form. The advantage of these rub-on preparations is their convenience. They can be carried in a parka pocket and applied as necessary. They do not provide the kind of protection offered by a hot wax, and rarely glide as well, but they are better than no wax at all. Never try to iron-in a wax designed to be rubbed. Rub-on waxes contain a soft, rubbery adhesive that turns to a sticky, gummy glop when heated. To glide at all, a ski covered with this gunk will have to be scraped down to bare plastic and rewaxed.

You'll also see various non-wax base preparations on the market, typically spray-on or wipe-on liquids containing Teflon or another PTFE material. Maxiglide is the best-known example. These bead water well, but they are incompatible with wax, so if you're going to use one, start with a clean, wax-free base. Some of the Teflon formulas wear off quickly—Teflon doesn't stick to anything very well.

5
Damage Control

While skis are very robust, they can be damaged by powerful impacts. In the fall and spring, we inevitably bounce our skis off rocks, leading to dings and gouges in bases and edges. The most common cause of heavy damage, however, is negligence.

Railing

Negligence leads to two conditions that will make good skis useless: railing and rust. Skis become railed when you fail to file them flat for any length of time. The plastic sole wears down, leaving the steel edges extending beyond the surface like the rails that freight trains run on. And a railed ski handles pretty much like a freight train. Cure railing with the biggest, meanest file you can find—a body file, perhaps—or take the skis to a good ski shop equipped with a wet-belt sander or stone grinder, and an expert who can run it without case hardening your edges.

Rust

Rusted edges result when skis are put away still covered with road grime, or when they're left wet inside a sealed ski bag. In addition to diesel oil, microscopic bits of asphalt, sulfur dioxide, and various unburned hydrocarbons, road grime is composed of a generous helping of road salt and other corrosive chemicals spread by highway departments to de-ice the roads. Road salt kills trees, and if you want to know what it does to ski edges, just walk into a local auto body shop and take a look at some rocker panels. The first thing to do when you take your skis off the top of your car is to wipe them down with a clean wet sponge. Wipe the bindings, too. Then store your skis in a dry, heated place, so they dry out properly.

Once ski edges are badly rusted, the only cure is a session with the wet-belt sander, which may take off enough material to shorten the life of the ski significantly.

Deep Gouges

Different types of damage can be done by impact, most frequently by the impact from skiing over rocks. Most of the time, you'll put a small ding or long striation in the base. Occasionally you'll tear out a hunk of plastic, right down to the fiberglass or aluminum backing of the plastic base. The worst gouges are close to the steel edge. If the edge itself isn't bent or separated from the body of the ski, patch the polyethylene base carefully to assure a good watertight seal. This prevents the edge from rusting out from inside the ski. When a large flap of base material is torn loose, the repair becomes tricky because polyethylene doesn't stick easily to anything but itself. In the ski factory, the base often has to be flame-treated on the bonding side in order to glue it permanently to the ski's structural layers.

When a base is torn this way, cut away the damaged part of the base and clean the underlying material thoroughly. Use emery cloth to clean and roughen the surface and clean it again with a strong detergent or wax remover—but not with benzene or any other agent that may etch the surrounding plastic or weaken its bond. Flush the

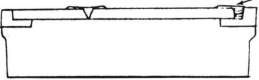

Fill very deep gouges in layers

Overfill each gouge, then scrape smooth

area thoroughly with clean water, and dry it thoroughly—a hair dryer will help. Then, using a high-quality epoxy, carefully laminate-in a sheet of polyethylene base material cut to fit the excised portion precisely. Most good ski shops are prepared to do this patch job. If you are not, you can make a semipermanent repair by dripping in several layers of P-tex candle. Build the layers up gradually and allow each layer to harden completely.

P-tex Candle

Ski bases made of softer grades of polyethylene—extruded bases of P-tex 1000 or similar materials, plus P-tex 1800—can be patched easily using P-tex candle.

The first step in repairing minor gouges is to clean the base with wax remover. Then inspect the base for rock damage. Dings and gouges should be repaired promptly, especially if they are near an edge; at the edge, they can act as a channel for water to seep through and rust the key slot anchors holding the edge in place. Use the point of a sharp knife blade to clean any dirt or old wax out of the gouges, and cut off any loose flaps or strings of plastic.

Choose one gouge to work on first. Place a sheet of metal—an old cookie tin or cheap aluminum pie plate—under the ski to catch any

Use a sharp knife to clean old wax and dirt from rock gouges, and cut away loose strings and flaps of polyethylene.

drippings from the P-tex candle. The candle will burn with a more subdued, controllable flame if you cut it lengthwise into four thin strips. Cutting P-tex candle is tough, even with a very sharp knife, and it's one reason most ski shop mechanics prefer to work with rolls of P-tex wire instead of the thick candles. Now place your steel scraper flat on the ski base to catch drippings alongside the gouge and light the end of the candle. This is easy to do with an ordinary wax table candle, which you can keep lit on a plate next to the ski— it's much harder to do with a lighter or kitchen match. With a wax candle burning nearby, you can relight the P-tex frequently as you move from gouge to gouge. But remember that some of the liquids you use around the workbench are flammable—don't use them near the open flame. This includes wax remover, many adhesives, and sprays.

When you first light the P-tex candle, it will burn yellow and cold, and you'll see big black flakes of carbon forming at the burning end. Turn the candle slowly and drip this cold burn off onto a steel or aluminum surface. After a minute or so, the candle will begin to burn with a low, hot blue flame, and the liquid P-tex will clear up, generating much less carbon. This clear material is the stuff you want to put into a gouge. Hold the burning end close to the gouge—you may touch the flame to the ski's base and flow the liquid into the gouge. Don't drip the liquid onto the gouge from above the base. In falling, the drips cool and carbonize. Work right on the surface of the ski.

The candle will flow slowly at first, and the liquid will congeal quickly. Keep turning the candle so it burns evenly and move it along the length of the gouge, flowing the plastic in to fill the ditch. If the gouge runs over the edge of the ski, don't worry. Just be sure the cookie tin is there to catch any drippings. Don't allow the molten polyethylene to drip on anything flammable, or on linoleum, or on your shoes or skin. The stuff is like napalm. It burns fiercely, and sticks as it burns. It will cool quickly, but meanwhile it hurts like hell.

The flame may soon begin to burn yellow again, and plastic will drip off the end of the candle much more quickly. At this point blow the candle out and start over with a cool one.

Overfill each gouge. The final hardened patch should be higher than the surrounding base material so you can plane it down to a level surface.

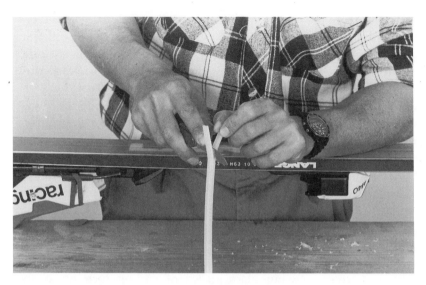

The P-tex candle will burn clean and evenly if you split it into quarters. That exposes more surface to the air, relative to the stick's volume, producing a hotter flame.

Light the P-tex candle from a steady flame. When it burns hot and clear, producing no flakes of carbon, flow it smoothly into the gouge. Keep turning the stick so it burns evenly.

Overfill the gouge. When the patch hardens, it should stand above the base . . .

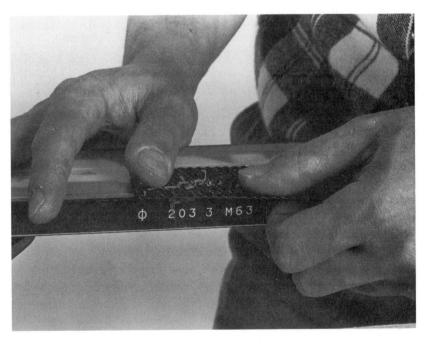

. . . so you can shave it down smooth with a Sur-form file.

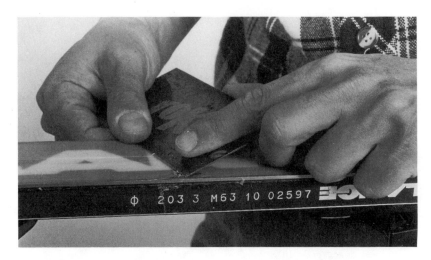

If you don't have a Sur-form file, use a sharp steel scraper to plane the patch down level with the base.

The plastic patches cool pretty quickly. As soon as they are hard, use a Sur-form file blade to flatten them. The Sur-form blade is like dozens of tiny wood planes. A couple of passes with a Sur-form produces a neat surface that blends almost invisibly with the surrounding material. Then get out your whetstone and file to do a quick flat-file and edge-file job, paying special attention to rock-damage burrs on the steel edge. Unfortunately, there is no way to fill rock gouges in the steel edge.

Sintered Base Repair

P-tex candle works well on extruded bases, which have a relatively low melting point. But candle rarely sticks well to the tougher sintered bases—candle patches generally pop out of sintered bases after a few runs or a few days.

Your ski bases are sintered if they are made of P-tex 2000 or 6000, or of HMW 3 or 6 material. Essentially, sintered bases are made of a higher quality polyethylene that has a much longer, tougher molecular structure. If the polyethylene molecule is less than a million atoms long, it can be melted and extruded. If the molecular weight is higher than one million, however, the plastic can't be melted without seriously degrading its molecular structure. In this case, the raw plastic powder is compressed into a big round solid block in a powerful hydraulic press. This non-melting solidification is called *sintering*. Any powder that's been compressed into a solid without melting is called a *sinter*. Most crusted snow has been sintered, for instance, and the process is often used to make tough metallic blends like automobile brake pads.

A sintered base has several advantages over an extruded base. First, because the molecules are longer, the plastic is tougher. It stands up better to rock damage and holds its shape longer after it has been structured. Because it contains fewer crystals and has never been in liquid form, it is also less dense—there are more pores to hold wax. That porosity has a negative side, though. If you allow the base to dry out, more air gets into the base and it oxidizes more quickly. Sintered bases have to be waxed more often.

P-tex candle adheres poorly to sintered bases because sintered plastic doesn't melt easily, so no good interface develops between the patch and the surrounding plastic. You can improve the chances for a good bond by superheating the material with a plastic welder or hot air gun—a minimum temperature for this kind of repair is 850° Fahrenheit. This kind of heat must be applied very precisely, because if you overcook the surrounding material you risk delaminating the base by melting its adhesive. Several companies make plastic welders designed to apply just this kind of controlled heat and pressure (see Appendix E).

A more permanent patch for sintered bases can be made with a hot air gun or plastic welder. Here the gun is set at 850° Fahrenheit, sufficient to melt P-tex wire and soften the walls of the gouge for a good bond.

P-tex Repair Sticks can be melted with a hot iron . . .

. . . to leave a smooth, clear patch. A milky color indicates a poor bond.

An easier way to patch a sintered base is with a semipermanent Repair Stick. Toko packages this material in flat strips, like plastic Popsicle sticks. It's a low-grade form of polyethylene that melts at under 200° Fahrenheit, so it can be liquified with a waxing iron. After cleaning out a base gouge thoroughly, simply use the tip of your waxing iron to melt and press into place the end of a Repair Stick. In this case, you are using the mechanical pressure of the iron to help force the semiliquid patch in and around the pores of the base material. The Repair Stick patch should be clear—a milky color means it's been overheated or underheated, and will probably pull out. Once placed properly, the patch is surprisingly durable, though it is slower and softer material than the sintered base around it. If you can't find Repair Sticks, try the soft plastic used to hold six-packs of soda or beer together. It melts easily and makes a good ironed patch.

Edge Repairs

Any ski repair becomes difficult if a section of edge has been damaged. Only a good ski shop will be equipped to remove a section of damaged edge and install a new, matching piece. If the edge has merely delaminated at the tip or tail, and curled up off one end, you can try to fix it at home.

Major edge damage is not always repairable. This ski may be patched for use in powder, but is now useless on hard snow.

Use a sharp knife to dig out any dirt between the plastic base and the ski's sidewall, then clean the exposed parts of the edge thoroughly with emery cloth. Pry the base back gently and clean the exposed bonding surfaces with a sharp point; scrape out any old glue left in the joint. Then fill the split with epoxy, working the glue in with a thin blade—a clam knife is ideal. Push the edge back into place, wrap the repair in wax paper to keep the epoxy from oozing out onto your clamps, and clamp the edge tightly to cure.

After the epoxy has set overnight, unwrap the ski and clean up any adhesive overflow with a file. There may very well be a bulge at the repair site. Flat-file and edge-file the ski to make this section uniform with the rest of the running surface.

Dents

A few skis with soft or brittle cores can be dented. For instance, some honeycomb skis can show a dented base because impact with a rock has bent the walls of the honeycomb structure under the impact point. You can't straighten out the core again, but you can fill the depression in the base. Roughen the plastic with emery cloth and melt the polyethylene candle into the dent in layers, the way you'd fill a deep gouge.

On a few skis it's possible to knock the aluminum tail protector out. It's a simple enough matter to clean the mating surfaces and epoxy the tailpiece back in, but it must be done promptly before moisture begins seeping through the exposed notch into the core. Damp cores rarely dry and will eventually rot, like an old wooden boat. If you have lost the aluminum tail bar, seal the open slot with a good epoxy. Use masking tape to build a dam around the slot and fill it with the epoxy.

Terminal Cases

A ruptured sidewall usually means serious structural damage has been done to the load-carrying layers of the ski. Check carefully for bends, warps or tiny cracks in the edges, base, and topskin. Check also for delaminations above and below the site of the sidewall break. The core may be broken. If you are convinced that the underlying fiberglass or metal layers are still in one strong piece, then you can seal the impact-damaged sidewall to prevent water seepage. Do this with epoxy, wax paper, and a clamp. However, if the ski's structural layers or core are damaged, the ski will almost certainly break the next time you start cranking turns. Clean it up and hang it over the mantle.

This brings us to the various reasons to retire a ski. Fatigue damage is something you can't do much about. The most common form is a bent ski. Sooner or later you'll see a metal sandwich ski with its tip pointing upward at an odd angle. It's possible to ski on a mildly bent ski for several days and not notice anything wrong, other than a worse-than-usual lack of coordination. If you have an older pair of skis, it pays to put both skis down on a flat surface from time to time, just to see if the camber and tip angle still look the same for both members of the pair. Sometimes this is the only way you can spot a bent shovel.

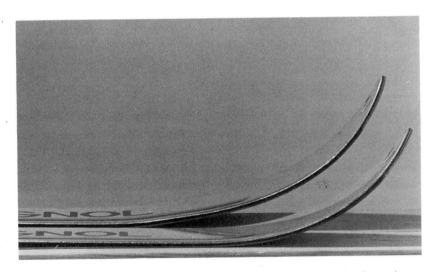

The far ski is bent. It can be bent back to shape, but the aluminum is permanently weakened and the ski will eventually bend again.

If you ski mostly in powder, you can bend a metal ski roughly back into shape and finish out the season on it. Bending the ski will help restore its turning characteristics, but the ski is still permanently weakened at the bend site and will inevitably bend again.

Metal skis can also delaminate. Sometimes delamination will show up as a bubble under the edge, usually at the front of the shovel where impacts occur every time you put the edge into a mogul or water bar. Small bubbles can be glued and clamped, just like a separated edge, but gluing a major delamination usually produces an impossibly stiff ski. These failures, along with spiral warping, are good reasons to hang 'em up.

After many years of use, skis simply wear out. Fiberglass skis grow steadily softer and softer in flex. When they no longer work in hard snow, you may get a few more seasons on them in powder. If the edges are still good, it's possible to replace the worn-out base of most skis. For $50 to $75, a major ski service center can rout out the old base and glue in a brand new polyethylene running surface. It's a good way to get another few years of service from a favorite pair of boards, but don't be surprised if the repaired skis are somewhat stiffer than the skis you sent in. Ask a good local ski shop where they send this kind of work. Have it done over the summer, since it involves shipping skis long distances.

Ski Shop Damage

It's not supposed to happen, but sometimes it does—a ski shop damages a ski while mounting the bindings. It usually involves delaminating the topskin by putting a long screw in a short hole, in which case the ski must be replaced. Sometimes the screw merely pushes out a top edge, which can sometimes be repaired. The shop should be responsible for repairing this kind of damage.

On thinner skis, particularly skis for kids, a shop will sometimes mount bindings with adult-size screws, which can punch right through the base or create pimples that push out the base. It's impossible to learn to ski with screws sticking out the bottoms of your skis. Inspect any new children's skis for these pimples. If you discover this condition long after the fact, simply remove the binding screws, grind the sharp ends off them, put a drop of glue into each screw hole, and reinstall the shortened screws. Then flat-file the ski to level out the bumps.

Wear and Tear

Topskin damage is more or less unavoidable unless your skis never leave the house, and since it's a cosmetic problem consisting of minor nicks and scratches, don't worry about it. Aluminum top edges should be inspected frequently for gouges, because they sometimes grow wicked metal splinters, which can cut a hand pretty badly. The guy who usually discovers these splinters is the guy who tunes the skis, so watch it. File these nasties down smooth.

As miles and years pile up, watch the top edges carefully, especially at the shovel and tail. If the core shows through, patch the worn spot immediately with epoxy to prevent water seepage. Cracks and crazing of the topskin are unimportant unless the fiberglass under the topskin begins to chip and peel. If the ski is still under warranty and a deep crack appears in the topskin, by all means return it for service. If it is no longer under warranty, and only the top sheet of ABS is cracked, patch it with epoxy and keep skiing.

Most good skiers don't worry much about the way the topskins look. "My students are always skiing across the tops of my skis anyway," one experienced instructor told me. "If the bottoms are slick, so am I."

Repairing Electra Bases

Many fast-gliding skis are now equipped with carbon-filled, sintered bases—one of this type is the Electra polyethylene base. Electrically conductive carbon-filled bases were originally developed to reduce static electricity in the chutes used to transport coal in mines, because sparks in the chutes could ignite the methane gas always present in coal-bearing rock. Ski makers discovered that the carbon-filled plastic was 3 to 5 percent faster than clear sintered bases in some snow conditions, but this is probably due to the lubricating quality of the carbon rather than to its anti-static properties.

These black bases should be tuned and waxed exactly like any other good sintered base, but patching them with ordinary P-tex candle or repair strip material leaves a section of base without the carbon additive. If it's a large patch, you may want to rub in Toko's Electra Additive carbon supplement. After sanding the patch flat and restructuring the base, rub in the additive as if you were applying shoe polish—the stuff comes out of its tube looking and smelling like shoe polish. Let it dry thoroughly before hot-waxing.

6
Storing and Transporting Skis

A fresh tune-up represents a lot of work. Don't risk ruining it by mistreating your skis in transit. Be sure the skis are tied together securely, allowing no chance of scissoring, which would ruin the careful polishing you've done on the edges. The skis should not only be locked together with the ski brakes, but also secured with a ski tie at the shovel. Racers protect the wax by placing newspaper or lint-free tissue between the skis.

Race Course Salt

In warm weather, race courses are protected from melting and rutting by hardening them with salt and other corrosive chemicals. At springtime race training camps, coaches spread salt on the courses every morning. The stuff gets on skis, bindings, boots, pants, sweaters, goggles, and gloves. Wash your gear with a garden hose every day after skiing a salted course, or face serious rusting and pitting of all metal surfaces.

Car Travel

It's most important to protect skis from road salt. When possible, travel with the skis inside the car, properly bagged to protect the upholstery and the occupants. Tie the ski bag down with the rear-seat safety belts so it won't shift around as you turn corners and brake.

If the skis must go on an external ski rack, bag them, even if that means just wrapping them with plastic bags. In fact, plastic bags have a big advantage over expensive nylon ski bags in that you can simply toss them out on arrival. You don't have to hang them, filthy and dripping, in the bathroom to dry.

Not every ski rack you can put on your car will accept a ski bag, but if you have invested $400 and many hours of work in your skis and bindings, it's worth paying an extra $20 or $30 for a ski rack that will do so. Or you can tie the ski bag to a bar-style rooftop carrier, using rubber bungee cords.

Skis travelling atop a car should be bagged for protection against road grime and salt.

Going by Air

Airlines, of course, require that skis be bagged. Take extra care with skis checked as luggage. Use a good, tough bag and tape the skis together with duct or strapping tape. Ski ties can break or snap loose from the rough handling bags get in busy airports, and the skis are likely to scissor when that happens. Remove anything attached to the ski that might break off—Parablacks and similar anticrossing devices rarely survive the journey.

Bindings take the most punishment in air transport, because baggage handlers will often drop huge piles of ski bags together in heaps, and the bindings get mashed; binding parts crack and break off mysteriously in airports. When you pick up your skis at the baggage claim, open your ski bag and check things like heel levers, brake arms, and toe pivot posts for bending and breaking (see Chapters 13 and 14). Airlines should be held responsible for the damage they do.

I usually travel with several pairs of skis. They all go in a single voluminous nylon bag that cinches tightly at either end to keep the skis bound securely together. When I arrive I can slide the bag into a hatchback rental car or, if the car is too small, I can tie the bag unopened on top. The bag is a unique color, and therefore easy to find when the airline sends it to the wrong state.

Packing Tools

Make up a small travelling ski-tuning kit consisting of one or two files, a plastic scraper and steel scraper, file cleaner, whetstone, Surform file, P-tex repair material, and a couple of bars of wax. The kit can be rolled up in a leather or cloth case, or in a shop apron. Stuff the tool bag in your check-through luggage. A 10-inch mill bastard file looks pretty strange in a carry-on bag, and unless you are prepared to spend an hour explaining to the security police why they shouldn't consider it a weapon, it's better off in the cargo hold. Don't pack it in your ski bag or you may arrive with a strange set of notches worn in your edges.

Storage

Skis should be stored in a dry, heated room, but not in an ovenlike attic or a damp basement. Tune and wax skis before storing them for more than a couple of weeks. The wax will prevent rusting. Tie them to prevent scissoring and stand them in a closet, secured so they can't fall over—a pair of falling skis can be lethal to

A traveller's ski-tuning kit consists of basic files, scrapers, whetstone, and repair materials . . .

. . . all rolled up in a protective leather case. It goes in the bottom of the duffel bag.

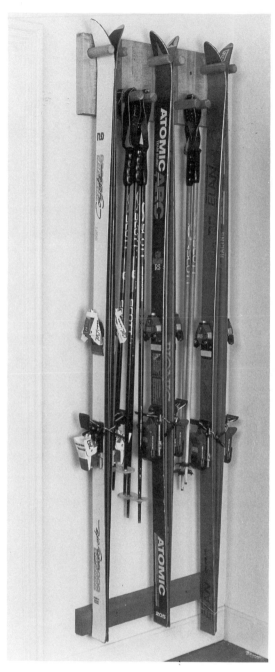

At home, skis should be stored where they won't fall over and where they can dry out.

an unwary person searching for galoshes. A single pair or two can be fastened up simply by putting a screw eye in the wall at shovel height and passing a cord around the skis and through the eye. A family recreation room or "mud room" is a perfect place to build a ski rack that will hold everybody's gear off the floor, out of the way, where it will stay dry and clean.

An advantage of the rec-room ski rack is that when skis are visible and easily accessible they are likely to be tuned more often. It's a good rainy day endeavor. If skis are buried in a closet, behind the coats and boots, they may be forgotten. You'll drag them out in a hurry while packing for the weekend and discover that the bases are unpatched and unwaxed and that the edges are rusting.

PART II
BOOTS

7
Boot Fit

The most important consideration in buying ski equipment is not ski length or binding adjustment. It's boot fit. If your boots don't fit correctly, nothing else will work properly—certainly not your carefully tuned skis—because all control of the skis has to pass through the boots. If your boots are too large, you lose some of the control you should have.

It is ironic that, while boots have improved vastly in materials, flex, design, and most recently shape, skiers still tend to buy boots that are too large. One problem is that each European manufacturer has a different idea of what an American size nine should be, another is that most factories design boots for an imaginary "average" foot. No skier in the world has an average foot, just as there is no such thing in the real world as a family with 2.3 kids. Typically, a skier walks into a ski shop, tries on two or three pairs of boots, and buys the most comfortable pair. Half the time, the boots are comfortable because they're too big. The skier gets the boots out on the hill, and as soon as he begins pushing against the leverage offered by a ski, he finds his feet rolling around inside his boots like a tin can on the floor of a car.

To get the most intimate contact with your ski, buy a boot with a shell that conforms as closely as possible to the shape of your foot. That means finding the smallest boot shell you can get your foot into comfortably. Then adjust the shell and liner until the boot is as snug as you can make it, but so comfortable you could fall asleep in front of the fire with the buckles done tight.

Start by measuring your foot. If you wear a size 9 street shoe, you may need a 7½ or 8 Nordica, an 8 or 8½ Raichle, a 320 or 340 Salomon, or a 7 or 8 Dachstein, depending on foot width and instep height—a fat foot may demand a larger boot. Another complicating factor is arch length, the distance between the heel and the widest part of the foot. If the Brannock device says you have a size 10 foot, but your toes are disproportionately short, your arch length may be that of a size 11 boot—and the size 11 is what you should ski in to put your heel and metatarsal where they should be in the boot shell. You'll have plenty of toe room, but the important parts of the foot will be snug and comfortable. A more serious problem is the foot with extra-long toes. Put that foot in a shell with the heel and ball of the foot properly accommodated, and the toes may have to curl up in front. The solution may be to go with a longer but narrower shell and push out the shell plastic at pressure points to accommodate the fact that the widest part of the foot is farther back in the boot.

Try on lots of boots. Nowadays most ski shops stock only two or three brands, so trying on six or eight different brands may mean visiting four or five shops. Do it. It's worth the time and trouble to get exactly the right boot.

Shop early in the season to take advantage of a full size range, especially if you have a very large or very small foot, and avoid busy holiday periods when sales clerks will have very little time and less patience to deal with a picky customer. A skier's best friend is an experienced boot-fitter. Deal with a shop you trust, one that offers a guaranteed fit.

As you try on boots, remember that most boots will stiffen in the cold, and also when locked into a binding, which reinforces the thin plastic sole. To ski efficiently, you need to be able to bend your ankle, which means flexing the boot. In the ski shop, lock the boots into a ski exercise machine or into a pair of bindings on a rental ski. Then lever around in them to see how they flex and how much your foot moves inside. If the boot feels too stiff in the warm shop, it will feel even stiffer outside in the cold. It can be made more flexible,

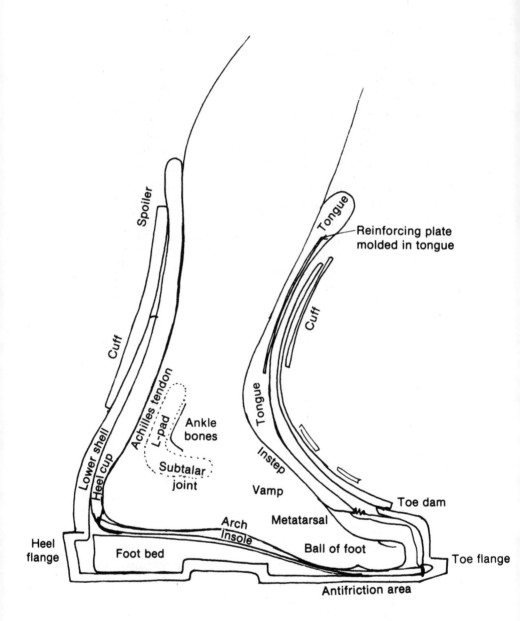

Parts of the Boot and Foot

but the problem may simply be that the boot is too big—the stiffness of any cylinder (the boot shell is really a foot-shaped cylinder) increases as the cube of its diameter increases. So, a boot that's just 5 percent too big may be 15 percent too stiff. A personal example: I can ski happily in a 7½ Nordica. I can't flex an 8½ even in a warm ski shop.

When you find a boot that seems to work, try it one size smaller just to be sure—always buy the smallest practical shell. Most boot companies build shells to full sizes, using a thicker liner to make up half sizes. In a borderline case, you're better off in the smaller shell with the thinner liner, because there will be less foot movement later as the liner beds down and because the boot will be easier to flex.

How Boots Should Fit

In the shop and on the hill, boots should fit snugly but not uncomfortably. Toes should wiggle, but the heel, instep, and ball of the foot should be effectively immobilized. There should be no pressure points over the instep, around the ankle, or against the shin.

"Hot spots" and pressure points along the sides of the feet, usually at the ball of the foot or along the outside of the metatarsal, can mean the boot is too narrow. The easiest solution is to remove some of the foam from the innerboot at the location of the painful spot. Boots with injection-molded foam inners are easiest to work on. Just slice the foam off in thin layers until the fit is right. With inners of sewn construction, make a door-shaped incision in the outer lining (usually made of vinyl-coated nylon fabric) and dig out the foam with a knife point or small screwdriver. If the boot has "flow fit," the puttylike or oily flow material will be contained in special plastic sacs inside this outer lining, usually around the heel and ankle. Be careful, as you cut into the lining, not to puncture the flow sacs. Once you have the hot spot reduced, close the incision with duct tape. Another way to adjust the narrow boot is to have the ski shop expand the shell over the pressure points. Every good shop is equipped to do this job quickly.

Cramps or pain over the instep, often accompanied by cold toes, mean your boots don't provide enough clearance over a high instep. This may be because you have an unusually high instep, or because

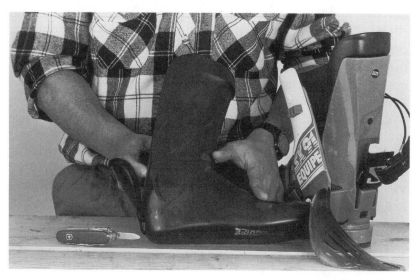

Pressure points can be relieved in molded innerboots by grinding or slicing away sections of foam. In this case pressure points have been relieved outside of the metatarsal, in front of the ankle, and alongside the Achilles tendon over the heel.

With a sewn innerboot, removing foam requires cutting the outer lining and probing inside with a knife.

you've overtightened a boot that is too large in an effort to keep your foot from sliding around. If it's an instep problem, relieve it by lowering the footbed. Pull out the plastic footbed from under the innerboot and shave it thinner.

A blister on your heel normally means the boot is too wide to immobilize your heel. As your foot moves inside the boot, the skin is rubbed raw. Add a cork heel wedge or a custom-molded insole to lift the heel into the narrower part of the boot's heel pocket, or tape padding around the heel area on the outside of the innerboot for a narrower fit. The latter solution is the better idea if you have a high instep to begin with, since adding a heel wedge can often make a boot tight over the instep. If you do add extra padding around the heel pocket, make sure it fits below the ankle or you'll create pressure points over the bony projections of the ankle.

Use adhesive closed-cell foam sheet, cut to fit, to fill space around narrow feet. Here foam is used to make a heel pocket narrower without adding pressure in the ankle area.

Cold toes with no additional pain or cramps means your boots are restricting circulation through the major veins near the surface of the foot. The two major vein systems under the skin in the foot are

along the top of the instep and on either side of the Achilles tendon.
It's very common to see boots cinched down hard over the instep,
and less common to see rear-entry boots with thick closure seams
shutting down the veins near the Achilles tendon. If your boot is
too tight over the instep, lower the footbed; if it's too tight behind
the ankle, remove foam from the Achilles tendon area, working in
vertical slices on the outside of the innerboot.

Most good ski shops carry a variety of boot-fitting aids, including
sheets of pressure-sensitive foam padding you can cut into the
shape you need to make a specific part of the boot narrower. A
recent innovation is specially shaped pillows of flow material with
sticky backs, designed to solve boot-fit problems quickly. But
remember that you can't relieve a pressure point by adding
padding. That only makes the pressure more severe. Relieve
pressure by removing material.

Rear-Entry Boots

Conventional boots and rear-entry boots present different types
of fitting problems. Conventional shells close down around the foot
as you tighten the buckles. There's less room to adjust for a high
instep or thick vamp, but less likelihood that the foot will roll
around within the shell. Most rear-entry boots, on the other hand,
arch high over the instep; for a time, many boot factories liked to
call these boots "volume fit" models. The problem here will be to
fill up that space over and around the foot without introducing a lot
of soft filler material that may not control foot movement well.
Some racers in rear-entry boots have been known to choose a boot
two sizes smaller, then pull out all the cables and filler materials so
they can jam the foot closer to the shell itself. That's a radical
procedure and requires that you tailor the innerboot very carefully
to solve all the fitting problems. As this book was going to press,
several boot manufacturers were considering the introduction of
custom foaming or flow-injection systems to fill the space over the
instep in rear-entry boots, but up to that time such systems had
made the boot fit so precisely that it became difficult to get the boot
on and off.

In the meantime, there is a lot you can do to a rear-entry
innerboot to fill more volume. Foam padding and special flow packs
are widely available; just slip the innerboot out, glue the additional

Conventional boots (left) and rear-entry boots (right) present different basic fitting problems. Conventional shells close down around the foot as the buckles are tightened. Rear-entry boots typically draw the foot away from the shell as the instep strap is pulled tight.

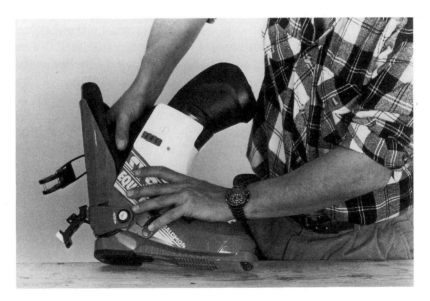

To remove an innerboot, reach deep to grasp the heel and pull it up and forward.

padding over the top of the innerboot like a saddle on a horse, and slide everything back into place, carefully relocating the internal pressure plate over the new padding.

Repairing the Tongue

Tongue problems are tough. There's very little you can do to make an ill-fitting tongue work better, and a tongue that is just a little bit off can do terrible things to tender shins. If your shins hurt, check the following:

- Are your socks or long johns bunched up in front of the shin? Use longer socks and pull them up tight. Also make sure your long johns don't end inside the boot, where their cuff seams can create pressure.
- Is the hard plastic reinforcing plate inside the tongue broken or separated from its foam backing? If so, the tongue should be replaced.
- Is the edge of the tongue curled under itself, or is it deformed from having been stored with the boot closed improperly? Try steaming it back into shape over a tea kettle. Wear gloves to keep from being scalded.
- Does the tongue bend over a fulcrum created by the shell top when you flex the boot forward? Try softening the shell flex, or reinforce the forward part of the tongue—the side that meets the shell—with a sheet of fiberglass or stiff plastic. A few products are designed to reinforce the tongue in this situation—typically, they consist of a piece of thermosetting plastic that is molded between your shin and the boot tongue, then baked hard to form a protective, formfitting shell. Ask a good boot-fitter to help with this operation, because it can be tricky. It's possible, for instance, to mold it so that the untrimmed edge of the shin guard itself becomes a pressure point, or interferes with boot flex.
- Some rough or sticky tongue materials simply rub the shin raw. Tape a plastic bag around the tongue to make a low-friction surface on the inside.

Custom Work

If it sounds as if buying a ski boot is just the starting point, you're right. Almost every professional skier I can think of has done something to customize his boots so they fit more precisely. The next time you take a ski lesson from an experienced pro, ask if you can take a quick look at the instructor's boots. Some of the fixes are extreme, and some very clever.

Because no two feet are alike, any strong skier will need to overcome the fit of a boot built for that fictitious average foot. Boot-fitters are used to seeing some very specific fit problems. Here are some of the most common:

- *The wide, muscular, athletic foot.* This foot usually grows on a very powerful leg with heavily muscled calves, which themselves create a fitting problem at the boot's spoiler. Most heavy feet belong to guys. Ski racers in their early twenties often have rigid feet with good arches. They need a wide-fitting boot shell (Koflach, Dachstein, Dynafit, sometimes Tecnica, Nordica, Munari, or Lange). As the athlete ages, the foot may spread and flatten, and bone spurs often develop. As the foot relaxes, it begins to pronate. A custom footbed becomes necessary, and it's also usually necessary to punch out the shell on the outside of the metatarsal or heel to accommodate odd protuberances.

- *The dancer's foot.* Dancer's foot is common among athletic women who have done a lot of gymnastics or modern dance in bare feet. The foot started off fairly narrow and with good musculature, but because the foot has supported a lot of pressure with little or no outside support, it has grown very wide and muscular around the ball—the foot is almost triangular, with a narrow heel and thick tough tissue in the metatarsal area. This skier needs a small, wide boot, often a junior racing boot (from Salomon, Nordica, Raichle, Koflach; also be aware that Lange makes special small and wide sizes for the Japanese market which can sometimes be special-ordered). It may be necessary to add thick, firm padding around the skier's narrow heel, and a custom footbed with a deep heel pocket will help compensate, too.

- *The high narrow foot.* Most high-performance ski boots are designed around a muscular foot. A skier with a healthy arch structure and high instep, but with a slender foot, will find few boots narrow enough to offer good support. Start with a narrower shell (Sanmarco Alpha, Raichle Flexon, or Caber Comp series) and a custom footbed to center the foot in the shell, then add padding as necessary.

A sensible approach to any unusual fit problem, especially for a strong skier who wants a very precise fit, is custom foaming. Almost all manufacturers now offer racing models with custom foam innerboots. The best of these innerboots have a leather outer lining, which conforms well to the contours of the shell. This leather lining can be expected to last years longer than a nylon liner because it stands up better to the abrasion from frequently being removed from the shell to dry.

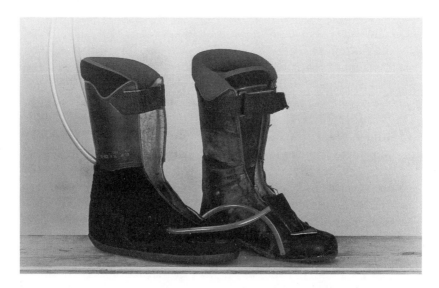

Ultimate solution to difficult fitting problems is the custom foam boot. At left is a nylon innerboot with foaming tubes. Foam is injected through the rear tubes and vents through the front tubes. Finished product, at right, is a leather innerboot that matches perfectly the shape of the shell and the shape of the skier's foot.

Custom Insoles

Before any custom work is undertaken on the shell, try to resolve fitting problems with a custom-molded insole. Several companies market these, chief among them: Superfeet and Peterson. A good ski shop can make a mold from the soles of your feet and create an insole to match it on the spot, or the shop can send the mold out to a lab to have the footbed made. A good footbed fits your foot as precisely as a contact lens fits your eye, and its purpose is the same: it corrects misalignments, allowing you both to feel the snow more sensitively and to control your skis more powerfully. The insole fills all the voids between the sole of the foot and the sole of the boot, so that every small movement of the foot is translated directly to the ski—there's no lag while the foot squishes down or rolls over to contact the inside of the boot shell.

Not everyone needs a footbed. Skiers who have naturally rigid feet with well-developed arches don't need this kind of support.

Starting point for any custom fit program is a custom-molded insole or footbed (left). Compare the accuracy and support provided by the custom footbed to a stock footbed from a good quality racing boot (right).

Most of us can use all the help we can get, especially after pounding our ankles and knees in other sports for years. By controlling the location of the heel within the boot and supporting both the arch and metatarsal areas, a custom footbed can make most skiers more comfortable in their boots and more controlled in their skiing.

A footbed can solve fitting problems for both wide-footed and narrow-footed skiers. It can cradle a wide foot, controlling the foot's tendency to push painfully out against the shell under pressure. And it can center a narrow foot, filling space and restraining the foot when it tries to roll around inside a boot that is too big. People with seriously broken-down feet, with flattened arches and a pronation problem, benefit the most from custom footbeds. A $50 or $70 footbed may solve 90 percent of boot-fitting problems right off the bat. So this is the place to start.

Boot Shell Adjustments

Most high-quality boots available today provide an important shaft cant adjustment, to angle the cuff laterally. Shaft cant adjustment allows you to match the cuff of the boot to the natural angle of your leg. If you look in a full-length mirror while wearing shorts, you're likely to see that your shins bow outward slightly— away from each other—when you stand straight; your ankles and knees are close together but there's some air between your calves. The amount of curve in the tibia varies across a fairly wide range,

Most shaft angle adjustments are made at the ankle hinge. Some use a simple screw mechanism, but many use an eccentric spacer system like this one. Note the shim at the back of the boot to adjust forward-lean angle.

but the lateral shaft cant adjustment lets you match the curve of your own legs so that your skis can glide flat on the snow when you stand in a neutral position.

To adjust the shaft cant, loosen the adjustment screw on the ankle hinge of your boot, put the boots on and stand on a hard, level surface, with your boots aligned in a natural skiing position—parallel to one another and about hip width apart. Do a couple of knee bends in the boots and come back to a neutral, flexed-ankle stance, just as you would stand on your skis in a schuss across very level terrain. As you hold this position, have a friend retighten the shaft cant screws, or, if the boot uses spacers to establish the proper cant angle, your friend can measure and fit the appropriate spacer into the eccentric hole at the ankle hinge for each boot.

Boots sold without shaft-angle adjusters can often be realigned by removing and relocating the rivets that function as ankle hinges. This is common practice on older Lange models, and any experienced boot-fitter can do the job quickly.

One easy way to experiment with subtle canting changes is to pad the innerboot. A layer of foam padding inserted between the innerboot and the shell on the inboard or inseam side of the cuff will place more weight on the inside edges of the skis. Padding on the outboard side will place more weight on the outside edges. A day of fooling around with sheets of foam can tell you whether you need canting and approximately how much. See Chapter 8 for more details on precise canting.

Most boots have additional shell adjustments, typically for forward lean and forward flex, and occasionally for footbed angle. Use these adjustments. Play with them as you ski. Make the adjustments in small increments between runs, or when you stop for lunch. After a couple of days of experimenting you'll find a combination of settings that is clearly the right formula—skiing will feel much easier and more natural at one group of settings than at any other. If you can adjust footbed angle, and if it doesn't affect instep fit too radically, try to elevate the back of the footbed as you adjust in more forward lean. Most skiers find that the boot is most sensitive and powerful when the foot and lower leg meet at a neutral angle around 88 degrees—close to a right angle. If you crank in a lot of forward lean without much forward slope to the footbed, you'll quickly bring the ankle angle well beyond that optimum range—to 85 degrees or less.

8
Making Boots Ski Better

Ski boot performance has improved so much since the beginning of this decade that it's almost safe to say that once all major fit problems are solved no more need be done to the boot. But many people still find themselves in boots that are too stiff or too soft, or are improperly canted, or that have too much or too little forward lean.

One of the great things about plastic ski boots is that they are easy to alter. Plastic can be cut and welded, softened and stiffened; rivets and buckles on plastic boots can be relocated. Before you begin any boot modification, have a good idea of what the change is likely to do to the way you ski. And bear in mind that a lot of ski boot characteristics are interrelated. Change the boot's neutral forward-lean angle and boot flex will change along with it. And you may find you'll have to change your footbed angle to match. So plan these alterations carefully, and rely on a good boot-fitter for expert advice.

Boot Flex

The most common skiability problem in boots that fit properly is that the boot is too stiff. Many lighter skiers often find they can't bend the ankle, and that forces them into an awkward rear-weighted position on the skis. If you bend your knees without bending your ankles, the result is a sit-down position ski instructors have indelicately labelled "the toilet turn." If you find yourself accused of hanging your butt out behind you, look first at your boots. Try opening the top buckle and see if that cures the toilet turn. If so, you need to soften your boots.

Most modern boots provide a flex control. If yours don't, you can still soften the flex. Any traditional overlap-style boot can be softened by drilling out the locking rivets and cutting flex channels in the lower shell. Many boots have flex channels molded in place, and all you have to do is cut along the dotted line with a sharp knife—after removing the innerboot, of course. Some boots even have snap-in inserts to stiffen the shell—just remove the insert, which may be well hidden under the cuff, and the boot will flex more easily. If the boot has no molded-in flex channel, cut a channel down the spine of the lower shell with a grinding wheel on a flexible shaft or Dremel tool.

The grinding wheel can also be used to feather a thinner edge in the overlapping surfaces of the front of the boot cuff, from the hinges all the way around to the ends of the buckle straps. You can also spray this area with a Teflon coating. Both tactics will help the cuff slide more freely over the lower shell, softening boot flex.

Boots with an external or "floating" tongue can usually be softened by grinding lateral flex channels into the external tongue or by grinding the tongue's edges thinner. Lubricate the tongue with a Teflon spray coating wherever buckle straps cross it. On Raichle Flexon series boots you can simply replace the tongue with a lower, softer version—the tongue screws off or pops off with a screwdriver. A Raichle dealer can make the switch in about 15 seconds.

Older Salomon boots, in particular the SX-90 models, are notoriously stiff in flex. Very few non-racers can bend them at all. Use your grinding wheel liberally on the detachable buckle strap that runs around the boot cuff—that strap provides most of the flex control. The front of the cuff can also be slotted laterally for softer flex.

Many boots can be stiffened in flex by adding locking rivets through the upper cuff and lower shell. Some bootmakers supply riveting kits with their racing models for this purpose, but an inexpensive pop riveter or a pair of tee nuts can do the job on older boots. The advantage of tee nuts is that the installation isn't permanent—if you don't like the boots stiff, the nuts come right out.

Forward Lean

Forward lean is closely related to forward flex. When you soften a boot, it usually means that you will naturally stand with the ankles bent a bit further foward—in effect, you've increased the boot's natural forward-lean angle or neutral angle, the angle at which the leg exerts no forward or backward pressure on the boot cuff.

In general, aggressive skiers like boots to put them in a more forward position, more relaxed skiers like to stand up straighter. Most modern racing boots can be adjusted to a neutral angle at around 18 to 21 degrees forward of a vertical position, which seems to be where most experts like the cuff to be. Softer high-performance boots are at a neutral angle at around 16 to 18 degrees, and boots designed for more relaxed recreational-style skiing are adjusted at more upright angles of 12 to 15 degrees.

Forward lean is also affected by the musculature of the calf. All else being equal, the skier with a dense, thick mass of muscle behind his tibia will be pushed forward more firmly against the front of the boot cuff by the calf, and that can add a couple of degrees to the forward lean angle compared to a slim-calved skier in the same boot.

It's easy to increase the forward lean of any boot without changing its forward flex. Just install a pad on the back of the innerboot. Make the pad of dense foam sheet, or cut a wedge of solid polyurethane or even cork, and tape it in place. This pad can also solve edge-control problems for skiers with slender calves by filling space that otherwise might allow the leg to roam around, like a broomstick in a bucket.

Most modern high-performance boots have built-in forward-lean adjustments, or permit easy adjustment by adding shims between the back of the cuff and the lower shell. Many traditional racing boots have a provision for resetting the locking rivets at the back of the cuff; you can change the spoiler angle, and therefore the neutral angle, of most rear-entry boots with a simple adjustment of the closure buckle or of its strap.

Canting

Chapter 7 discussed lateral shaft angle as part of boot fit. Canting is distinct from shaft angle. When boot-fitters talk about canting, they usually mean an adjustment made to the sole of the boot rather than to the angle at which the cuff meets the lower shell. Canting adjusts the angle of the foot to the ski, rather than the angle of the leg to the foot.

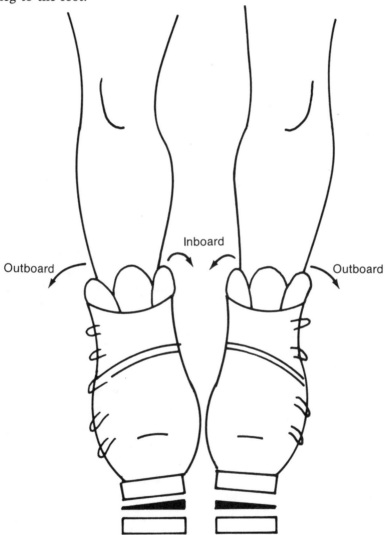

If you naturally stand on your outside edges, add cants or wedges with the thick edges *inboard*.

Fifteen years ago, when ski coaches first began talking about canting or wedging, boots were crude by modern standards. The industry was still experimenting with plastic, trying to come to terms with a material that offered incredible rigidity and therefore tremendous edge control. But the most pressing problems of the day were fit problems. For instance, plastic didn't break in the way leather did, so unless the plastic shell resembled a foot fairly closely, skiers finished the day by pouring blood out of their boots. Also the boots of the time made no allowance for the outward curve of the leg, so most skiers tended naturally to stand on the outside edges of their skis. This meant that the skis felt unstable—they wandered apart in straight running. The skier had to exaggerate the edging motion to drive the inside edge of the ski into the snow in a turn.

At the time, ski shops remedied this situation by installing wedges or cants under the skier's bindings, to put the ski flat on the snow when the skier assumed a natural, relaxed stance. Within a few years, bootmakers began building boots with a designed-in cant, ranging from half a degree to five degrees. At the upper end of this range it was not unusual to find skiers who were overcanted in their new boots, so that they tended to stand naturally on the inside edges of their skis. Standing thus, they had no difficulty beginning turns, but they did have trouble trying to end turns. And they crossed their tips a lot. Again, the solution was to install cants under the bindings, this time with the thick side of the cant over the outside edges of the skis to compensate for overcanting in the boots.

Today most good skiers with relatively normal legs, skiing in boots with properly adjusted shaft angles, can adjust automatically for a couple of degrees of cant—you may make an adjustment that big when you change boots. If the new boots are radically different in cant angle, however, you may find skiing awkward until you compensate for the change with a new custom insole or by installing wedges. Racers are even more sensitive. Some coaches say that even young racers can feel one-half a degree of difference in cant.

Cants installed under the bindings have an important disadvantage in terms of convenience—you can't switch your right ski for your left to equalize wear and tear on the edges. If, for reasons of anatomy, you need more cant from your boots than the manufacturer provides, ask your boot-fitter to grind the cant into the boot soles. It's a fairly straightforward procedure. He'll use a joiner to plane the boot soles to the correct angle, then fill the binding flanges at toe and heel with a polyurethane compound and trim them to restore the toe and heel to standard parallel surfaces for proper mating with the bindings. Because binding-release characteristics are affected in this operation, grinding the soles to establish cant should be left to a professional.

9
Boot Maintenance

Mildew can be a problem if boots are stored with wet liners. After each day of skiing, pull the inners out of your boots and let them dry overnight at room temperature. To keep the innerboots from cracking, splitting, deforming, and even melting, keep them away from direct heat, which means away from the fireplace and from baseboard heaters.

A boot drying rack, with pegs for hanging innerboots and a tray to hold the dripping from outer shells, is a handy item. Make one to organize the family's wet stuff. It can also accommodate soggy gloves, hats, and goggles. When my innerboots are very wet I bend a wire coat hanger to hold them, and hang them up where the air circulation is good.

Frequently sliding the innerboot out of the shell creates a significant amount of wear, especially at the seam where the bottom of the innerboot meets the heel. Cover this seam with a bead of silicone caulk and let it cure to form a protective coat. Renew the bead whenever it begins to wear thin.

Most of the flexible plastics used for boot shells have a molecular memory. They tend to hold a shape once that shape is set. For this reason it's important to buckle boots before storing them, even overnight. Otherwise the shells may "freeze" in the unbuckled position and distort slightly when it comes time to buckle them up again.

Minimize boot sole wear by slipping on a pair of Cat Tracks or similar oversoles before taking off across the parking lot. Always clean dried mud off of boots before storing them or before stepping into bindings.

As boots age, the toes and especially the heels do wear down. Nylon boot shells behave worse in this respect than polyurethane or polyether shells, but they all do it. Nowadays many boots come equipped with replaceable rubber sole elements at these heavy wear

Serious sole wear is evident on boot at right. When the sole is this badly worn, it begins to affect edge control and binding performance.

positions. The rubber pads screw on. Replace them regularly, before the screws are damaged. The important point about preserving boot sole shape is that you are preserving efficient binding performance. As the boot sole wears thin at toe and heel, the bindings have less material to grip, so retention and edge control are degraded.

After a long period of storage you may find that your boot fit has changed. Boots that contain pockets of flow material are usually the culprits: the flow material settles to the bottom of the pocket over a period of time. Gently warm the inside of the boot with a hair dryer to soften the flow material, and knead it to redistribute it throughout the ankle, heel, and instep areas.

Keep boots warm in transit. If they have to travel in the trunk of your car Friday night, bring them indoors to warm up before trying to get into them Saturday morning. Put a boot on warm and it will stay warm. Put it on cold and it may be too stiff to buckle. Worse, in winter weather the inside of the boot will never warm up properly, and you'll freeze your toes.

You can avoid most buckle damage by making sure the lower buckles are always closed, whether you're skiing or travelling. An open buckle lever is easy to snap off. Some buckles are placed in such a way that heavy powder snow can lift them open. You can grind the ends of the buckles so they will lie flat against the boot shell, or place a flap of duct tape in front of the buckle to keep snow from getting underneath it.

Repairing Boots

Boots wear out. It's as simple as that. I ski about 100 days a year and it's not uncommon to see a pair of brand-new boots go to hell in that period of time. Innerboot padding beds down so the boots seem to grow too large; tongues split or deform; soles wear out from walking, especially at the heel, so they no longer fit in a binding; buckles bend or break off; cables fray and break; shells split. Some models seem to self-destruct; others, properly cared for, soldier on for years.

Solve innerboot wear the same way you would treat a fitting problem, by taping closed-cell foam sheet to the outside of the innerboot to restore the boot's original fit. This is tough to do if the boot was originally lined with fleece or fake fur, because as those materials wear down you can easily lose a full size. Fortunately, no one lines boots with those materials any longer.

Split liners can be taped over or delivered to your local shoe repairman for a neat stitch-up. Be sure that the fit of the innerboot won't be affected by any stitched repairs.

When you've worn out the toes and heels of an older pair of boots, a pair that is not equipped with replaceable rubber pads at high-wear areas, the original shape of the boot can be restored by a good ski mechanic with a plastic welder. Split shells can be repaired using the same tool.

Minor leaks—at the toe dam, around the bottom of the cuff, or around the edge of an external tongue—can be sealed with silicone caulk or duct tape. If you ski in a lot of powder in a favorite pair of old boots, you may find it necessary to reseal the toe dam frequently. To keep that rubber toe dam from drying out in the first place, use Armor-All or silicone spray regularly.

Broken buckles are common, but easy to repair. Drill out the old rivets and install a new buckle with pop rivets or tee nuts. Any good ski shop can sell replacement buckles and will also install good-as-new rivets for a dollar or two.

PART III
BINDINGS

10
Mounting and Adjusting Bindings

This chapter describes in general terms how ski bindings should be mounted and adjusted. The information is provided so that you can inspect your own bindings and spot trouble—misalignments, misadjustments, damaged parts, and so on. The chapter is not a guide on how to mount your own bindings. Mechanically, the skills involved in binding mounting and adjustment are well within the range of a competent home mechanic—if you can fix your own small appliances you should be able to mount bindings safely. But—and it's a big but—bindings are critical to skier safety. If someone gets hurt skiing on a binding you have adjusted or worked on, you may be liable to pay damages in today's litigious climate. The mounting and adjustment of ski bindings should be left to ski shop technicians who have been trained and equipped by factory reps and who are covered, in case a customer is injured, by the binding company's liability insurance.

Binding Location

International standards call for boot soles to conform to a specific shape in order to work properly with bindings. Part of that standard calls for boots to carry a midsole mark embossed halfway along the boot sole length. Bindings should be located on the ski in such a way that the midsole mark on the boot lines up with a midsole mark engraved on the ski top or sidewall.

Some ski makers prefer to mark the location of the boot toe rather than the midsole point. The reason is that all these marks are designed to put the metatarsal of the foot over the midpoint of the ski's running length. The *running length* is usually defined as the length of base in contact with the snow when the ski is running straight on a flat surface—in other words, the running length excludes the ski's turned-up tip and tail sections.

The midsole mark system works well for most medium-size boots and feet, but often misplaces very large or very small boots. Placed on the midsole mark, a small boot can put the metatarsal well behind the running-length center, and a large boot can end up located too far forward. So some ski makers mark a scale on the topskin. Volkl skis, for instance, provide a scale running from 2 to 12, and you pick the midsole point from this scale according to English boot size. A U.S. size 9 is roughly a 7½ or 8 English, so if that were your boot size you'd locate the midsole of the boot over the 7½ mark on the ski. K2's midsole marks run from 22 to 35, and the numbers refer to boot sole length in centimeters. Measure your boot sole from toe to heel; if it's 30 cm long, for instance, you'd locate the midsole mark over the 30 on the ski-top scale.

This is all very complicated, but it's important. Mislocating the boot on the ski changes ski performance dramatically. Put the boot an inch too far forward, and the ski becomes unstable—it wants to turn, turn, turn and won't track quietly. It will also tend to dive like the *Titanic* in deep snow. Put the boot too far back and it gets too stable—trying to turn becomes like reaching forward to steer a bus from the back seat.

People with very small or very large feet should be concerned that a mechanic makes allowance for boot size in calculating binding location, and so should people who, for reasons of unusual arch length or other fitting problems, have the metatarsal located fore or aft of its usual location in the boot. If the metatarsal falls more than about 1 cm away from its normal position on the ski, it can make a noticeable difference in ski performance.

Drilling and Tapping

Binding screws come in two standard lengths, both with the same standard diameter and thread pitch. The longer screw is for adult skis, the shorter screw for kids' skis. To prevent delamination of the ski or screw pull-out while skiing, the screw holes must be drilled to the appropriate width and depth. Specifications for the screw holes vary according to ski-maker and binding factory directions, but typically a fiberglass ski should take a 3.5 mm diameter screw hole, and an aluminum or aluminum/fiberglass ski a 4.0 mm hole. Depth is usually 7.5 mm for junior skis, and 9.5 mm for adult skis. The screw holes should be countersunk about 1 mm to prevent topskin bubbling as the screw is seated.

In addition, metal skis and most foam-core skis need to be tapped, using a tap that matches the thread of the binding screws. Failure to tap the screw holes can cause delamination or screw stripping. The technical manual published by the ski manufacturer will contain specific instructions for tapping, along with advice on locating the binding retention plate built into the ski structure.

Screw Hole Location

Ski shop mechanics use special drilling jigs supplied by the binding factories to locate screw holes accurately. Screw holes must be centered within about .5 mm accuracy. This is difficult but not impossible to do without the drilling jig. One way to do it is to tape the binding itself in the correct position on the ski, then use a center punch to mark each screw location. It's especially important that the binding be centered properly between the edges of the ski. A misaligned toe unit, for instance, won't release properly.

Screw location becomes more difficult when relocating a binding, or installing a new binding on an old ski with old binding holes. Old binding holes should be sealed solidly with wood or plastic plugs, coated with epoxy, and driven tightly into each hole with a hammer. Golf tees make good plug material. Once the epoxy cures, the new holes can be drilled safely even if they overlap the old holes.

Seating Binding Screws

Binding screws are driven with Posidrive screwdriver bits. A Phillips #3 bit looks similar, but will strip the screw or damage the bit when driven with sufficient torque to seat the binding properly. Proper torque is typically about 20 pound-inches.

Difference between Posidrive bit (left) and Phillips #3 bit is subtle but important. Posidrive bit has thicker, square-cornered flanges. Using a Phillips bit on binding mounting screws will damage the screws or the screwdriver.

Seal the screw by putting a drop of wood glue in the screw hole before sinking the screw. The glue lubricates the screw threads going in, and dries to provide a watertight seal and to prevent the screw from vibrating loose. Epoxy works in most skis, but will make removing the screw impossible if the binding later needs to be replaced because of mechanical damage, and some epoxy glue can damage certain foam cores. On the other hand, some hollow-core and honeycomb-core skis need an epoxy potting glue to hold the screws firmly. See the ski factory's technical manual for specific recommendations on screw retention glues.

Forward Pressure Adjustment

The heel unit contains springs that push it forward along its track to press the boot into the toe cup, and this forward pressure must be set correctly. Inadequate forward pressure may allow the boot to pop out of the binding unexpectedly. Excessive forward pressure can impede initial movement, then force the boot out of the toe unit abruptly once the high starting friction is overcome. Both conditions are dangerous.

Put the boot in the binding. Forward pressure is correct when the index mark on the heel housing lines up between the appropriate marks on the heel track.

Adjust Salomon racing bindings by turning the lower screws at the bottom rear of the aluminum heel housing. Forward pressure is

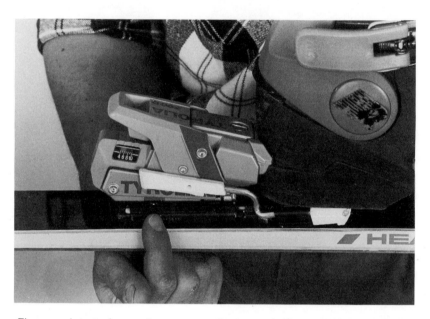

Finger points to forward-pressure adjustment indicator, here centered between index marks to show that forward pressure is correctly set. The screw on top of the heel cup adjusts heel-cup height.

correct when there is 1 mm clearance between the back of the screw and the heel housing, with the boot in the binding. Adjust other Salomon bindings by lifting the metal latch tab at the bottom rear of the plastic heel housing with a screwdriver blade. With the tab lifted, slide the heel housing fore and aft until you find the proper position.

On Tyrolia bindings, the heel housing is locked to its track by a screw just behind the ski brake treadle. Remove the boot from the binding to find the screw. Rotate this screw one quarter turn and lift the brass tab that sticks out beneath the brake treadle. Now the heel unit is free to slide on its track. Move the unit to its proper position and press the tab back down. Rotate the screw back to its locked position and replace the boot in the binding. The brass index arrows on the lower rear sides of the heel housing should align between the hash marks.

On Marker bindings, forward pressure should coordinate with the binding's release setting. On turntable models, with the boot in the binding, turn the two screws at the ends of the heel springs until the index marks line up with a number corresponding to the selected release setting. On older step-in models, with the boot in the binding, turn the screw at the bottom rear of the heel housing until the index mark lines up with the number corresponding to the release setting. On current models turn the screw until the index marks line up on the side of the heel housing.

On Look turnable bindings, with the boot in the binding, turn the two screws at the ends of the steel diagonal arms until the back edge of the turntable platform aligns with the index marks below the platform.

On Geze bindings, with the boot in the binding, turn the screw at the bottom rear of the heel housing until the back face of the housing lines up between the index marks on the screw.

Toe and Heel Cup Adjustment

Toe- and heel-cup height and width adjustments are critical to good edge control and smooth release. Some bindings are self-adjusting for these clearances.

The toe cup should not clamp down tightly on the boot toe. Instead, there should be .5 to 1 mm clearance. Check this by pulling backward on the boot spoiler to lift the toe, and slide a thin plastic card between the boot and the antifriction pad. Now tighten the toe-cup height screw or screws until the card can be pulled free with only slight friction resistance. Salomon, Tyrolia, Geze, and Look bindings have one toe-cup height adjustment screw; older Marker and Geze bindings have two, one on each toe wing.

In addition, some Salomon, Look, and older Geze models need to be adjusted for toe-cup width. On Salomon and Look bindings, look for a butt plate in the center of the toe cup. The boot toe should just kiss this butt plate. Using the screws on either side of

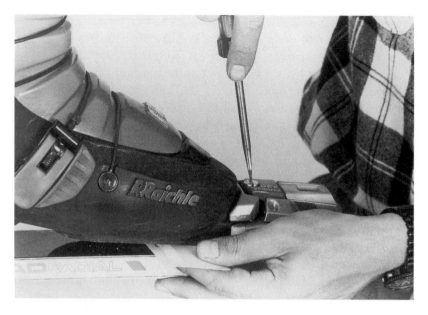

Adjusting proper toe-cup height requires use of a clearance gauge, in this case a thin plastic card. Slide the card between the boot sole and antifriction pad. Tighten the toe-cup height screw until you feel resistance on the card.

the toe wings, adjust toe-wing width until the butt plate clearance is correct. This will change the boot's fore-and-aft position, and require readjustment of forward pressure at the heel. Some older Geze models have a single screw on top of the binding, between the toe wings, which can be used to select one of three toe-cup width positions.

Nowadays only Tyrolia heels have a heel-cup height adjustment. Heel-cup height is correct when the ski brake treadle is fully depressed, but no excessive clamping pressure is applied to the heel.

Release Adjustment

All bindings use a common scale, defined by the German Industrial Standards organization (DIN), to measure release torque. The scale is in decaNewton-meters of torque, measured from the heel of the boot in lateral release. It's an approximate scale, and depends to a large extent on boot sole length to get a reasonable torque level.

Choose a release value based on body weight and height, skiing skills, age and sex, and boot sole length. See the binding manufacturer's adjustment table for your exact DIN scale setting. In general, adult male intermediate skiers should fall in the range DIN 5 to 7, experts in the range 6 to 10, racers 8 to 15. Adult women intermediate skiers may wind up with adjustment values of 3 to 5, experts 4 to 7, racers 6 to 13. Kids and adult beginning skiers should select lower values.

Release values are adjusted by turning the large screws at the front and back of the toe and heel units. DIN scales are clearly marked in windows on the toe and heel housings. In general, the numerical settings at toe and heel should be matched, though very strong skiers often choose a higher setting at the heel to reduce the incidence of unwanted release.

Caveat

It is very important to recognize that binding performance is a compromise between retention and release characteristics. At lower speeds and on flat terrain, safety usually lies in the direction of easier release. But at high speeds and on steep terrain, a skier may often have a better chance of avoiding injury if the possibility of unwanted binding release is greatly reduced.

Binding manufacturers take this trade-off into account in calculating suggested release values. But the release values themselves are worthless if the binding is improperly mounted, adjusted, or lubricated. These jobs should be referred to qualified mechanics.

11
Testing Bindings

Mounting and adjusting bindings may not be a job for the home workbench, but function testing is something any skier can and should do regularly. *Function testing* is a fancy term for working the binding to see if there's anything radically wrong with it. It's a form of cheap insurance, a troubleshooting procedure that tells you early if your bindings have been damaged or if boot sole wear is reducing binding efficiency.

Workbench Testing

At home, cycling the binding through its release modes is easy to do on the bench, and it's a good idea to do it several times each season, perhaps before any major ski-tuning effort.

Clean and dry your boots, skis, and bindings. Put the ski in your vise and try to rock the bindings on the ski. If there is any lateral play, inspect the mounting screws to see if any of them has vibrated or pulled loose, or if a screw or pivot post has broken or bent. Inspect the antifriction pad and the insides of the toe and heel cups carefully. Look for damaged or pitted low-friction surfaces. Many of these bearing surfaces are lined with Teflon plastic, a relatively soft material that may have torn or scored. If one of these surfaces

Nothing wrong with this toe-piece, except a loose screw. Right hand mounting screw has backed out. It can lead to poor edge control as the binding rocks on the ski, and by digging into the boot sole, it can impede release. With additional strain placed on the remaining screws, chances of a screw pull-out are increased.

The damaged antifriction pad must be replaced before this binding is safe to use.

has been damaged or contains embedded dirt, plan to take your skis to a ski shop to get the bearing surface replaced.

Now lock the boot into the binding. Rock the boot on the ski. If there is excessive movement, suspect that the boot sole has worn thin, or the toe- and heel-cup adjustment screws have vibrated loose. In either case, it's necessary to restore the proper clearances in order to regain good edge control. Also check that forward pressure is correct by looking at the index marks on the heel unit. Boot sole wear can affect forward pressure, too.

Now push the boot toe sideways until it moves half an inch in the toe binding. Release it and it should snap back to a centered position on the ski. Try this in both directions. If the boot does not return to center, spray the boot sole and toe and the insides of the binding toe and heel cup with silicone spray and try the test again. If it still doesn't work properly, a binding mechanic should investigate why.

Now push the boot toe sideways until the toe unit releases. Release should be smooth and progressive on both sides, to the right and to the left. Put the boot back in the binding and use the heel operating lever to release the boot heel upward. Do this slowly and watch the heel come up. Everything should work smoothly at the heel cup. Make sure the ski brake operates smoothly, and that its arms aren't bent.

Give the binding a careful visual check, looking for bent, damaged, and corroded parts. If everything looks good, go skiing.

On-hill Testing

Strong skiers frequently test bindings by self-releasing. It's not a good idea to do this every time you get out of your bindings, because it does twist the knees unnaturally, but once a week or so it's a good idea to simply twist out of the toe unit to assure yourself that you can do it. If your legs are stronger than your binding release springs, the bindings aren't likely to hurt you.

Don't try this at the heel. Many strong skiers can self-release upward from the heel, but there are also cases on record of skiers injuring their ankles and Achilles tendons trying this. Upward heel release should be tested in a properly equipped ski shop, on a machine.

12
Binding Maintenance

Bindings are pretty rugged, and most major maintenance operations should be undertaken by qualified mechanics. But primary responsibility for preventing mechanical damage and corrosion rests with the skier.

If you take good care of your base and edges, corrosion probably won't be much of a problem. The bindings are along for the ride, and if you bag your skis to keep road salt off them, wash race course salt away with clean water, and dry the skis thoroughly after they come in from the snow, the bindings will also be salt-free and rust-free. Once bindings are dry, you can help prevent future water damage by spraying them regularly with silicone spray.

Impact damage can bend binding parts. Check your bindings regularly for bent posts and especially for bent brake arms. A badly bent ski brake may not deploy, leading to a runaway ski. Brake arms can be bent whenever skiers collide with obstacles or tangle with one another, and the arms are particularly vulnerable when skis are stacked, *en masse*, in a base lodge ski rack. Some bozo knocks the pile down, and all those skis crash together, locking and twisting brake arms against each other.

Certain binding parts are designed to wear out and be replaced regularly. The Teflon antifriction pads and bearing sufaces inside the toe cup should be disposed of and replaced, like the air filter in your car. Get a mechanic to replace these whenever they look worn.

Use a silicone spray frequently to reduce friction and to protect binding parts from corrosion.

13
Major Binding Repairs

Major disasters happen to bindings. They strip screws. Once in a while an airline will break off an operating lever or bend a pivot post. Plastic covers are lost from toe housings and release adjustment scales.

Stripped Mounting Screws

When a binding screw pulls out or vibrates loose, remove it and unscrew the binding from the ski so you can get at the damaged screw hole. If the hole is undamaged, you can simply put some glue in it and reseat the screw. If the hole has stripped out, it must be plugged and redrilled. Shred some steel wool and push the metal fibers deep into the hole. Then mix up some epoxy and drip it into the hole. Make sure the epoxy and steel fibers mix thoroughly and fill the hole completely—stir around in the hole with a matchstick until all the air bubbles are out. Let the steel wool plug cure overnight, then redrill and tap the hole and reinstall the screw.

Occasionally a screw pull-out delaminates the ski. See Chapter 5.

Major Parts Broken

There's nothing you can do to repair a broken operating lever, bent pivot post, or cracked toe or heel cup. If the failure occurred during normal skiing, the binding should be replaced under warranty. Another warranty situation is a stripped adjustment screw—once in a while the steel screw that regulates toe-cup height or width will strip out of its softer aluminum or plastic channel, usually because it was originally cross-threaded by the automated machinery that assembles bindings in the factory. Most of the time, stripped screws are spotted by the mechanic who adjusts the bindings, and the skier himself never sees them. If you discover a stripped screw, see your dealer.

Bindings broken in transit, either by airline mishandling or in parking lot accidents, are not strictly the responsibility of the binding manufacturer. Ask your dealer about the cost of replacement parts. In today's market, it often makes more sense to replace a complete toe or heel unit than to disassemble it and replace only the broken parts.

Minor Parts Broken

Bindings often function well with minor plastic parts missing, but when you lose a plastic housing cover or brake arm sheath, plan to replace it anyway. Housing covers usually are there to help seal the binding mechanism against water entry. Getting lots of snow in the spring-cam mechanism can bind up the working parts with chunks of ice, reducing the binding's release efficiency, and water inside the binding can eventually create corrosion problems. So when you lose a plastic cover, use duct tape to cover the openings in the housing until you can get to a ski shop and buy replacement parts.

The plastic ends on your ski brake arms are there primarily to keep the steel wire from puncturing flesh. Bare wire ski brakes also do considerable damage to car-top paint, upholstery, and neighboring ski bases. So replace the plastic guards in the rare cases when they get knocked off.

Antifriction pads (AFD) are often designed to snap off easily, for quick replacement. But this means they sometimes snap off or break off when skiing, especially if they were improperly installed. Don't try to ski with an AFD missing. Bindings don't function properly without them.

Runaway Straps

Runaway or safety straps have almost disappeared from ski hills, replaced by ski brakes. It's a good thing—windmilling skis, held near falling skiers by straps, may have accounted for 15 percent of all ski injuries before ski brakes became common.

Nonetheless, there are situations when you want a strap on your ski, even if it's just a long cord to help you find a lost ski in deep snow. Most binding-makers provide an attachment point on the heel unit for a powder cord, though it usually requires some modification of the heel.

On Salomon bindings, find the hole in the steel substructure of the operating lever and drill through the lever's polyurethane cover to attach a powder cord. On Tyrolia bindings the cord can be looped through the existing hole on the heel lever. On Look and Marker turntables, tie the cord to the diagonal rods. Marker and Geze offer special steel shackles which can be attached to the heel by removing a mounting screw. Check with your dealer for availability.

PART IV
POLES AND GOGGLES

14
Pole Repair

Poles are simple, and pole repairs are simple. Aluminum poles either bend or break. The straps wear out or break. The baskets break or slip off.

Pole shafts come in several grades. At the top of the heap are the hard, springy, lightweight shafts made of seamless 7001 alloy, containing a lot of magnesium and zinc. These metals make the alloy very strong and stiff, but they also make it brittle. 7001 shafts are very difficult to bend, but when they do deform too far they fracture with a clean, sharp break. A broken 7001 shaft cannot be repaired.

Most good quality poles today are of a slightly more malleable 7040 or 7020 aluminum, rolled into a tube and welded. These shafts are somewhat heavier than 7001 shafts, but are equally strong and will bend instead of shattering. Cheaper poles are made of 6000-series alloys, softer still and easier to bend.

A moderate bend can be repaired. Wrap the pole with duct tape just below the bend and lock the tape-cushioned part in a heavy vise. Wearing gloves and safety glasses, grasp the end of the pole firmly and bend it back straight. Be careful and watch for any signs of breaking. The metal is permanently weakened at the bend site and you can expect it to bend there again. Eventually it will break after repeated repairs. If you need more leverage to bend a pole back straight, remove the grip and slip a length of pipe over the end of the shaft.

Baskets are easy to replace. Remove the old basket by slipping a pair of pliers over it and, with the pole point on a piece of scrap wood, striking sharply on the pliers with a hammer. Install the new basket by slipping it on the pole. Place the point of the pole in a hole

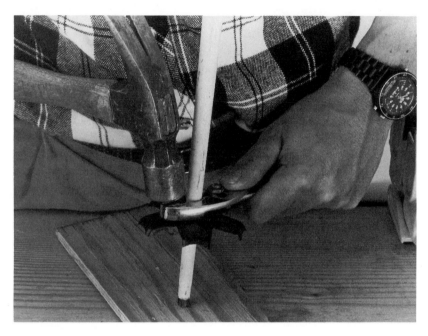

Remove pole basket by slipping a pair of pliers loosely around the pole shaft and striking it with a hammer.

drilled in a two-by-four and smack the top of the pole grip a couple of times with a rubber mallet to drive the basket on tight.

To replace a broken or worn-out strap, remove the Phillips-head screw from the top of the grip. Now the strap will pull out of its slot easily. Stick a new strap in, line up the brass grommet with the hole in the grip, and replace the screw. Some poles use a snap-in anchor for the strap. Remove the anchor by prying it out gently with a screwdriver.

To remove a pole grip, simply twist hard and pull. Most grips can be pulled off by hand. A recalcitrant grip can usually be removed by

Install a pole basket by slipping it in place, then put the pole point in a drilled hole and hit the top of the pole with a mallet.

taping the shaft, putting it in a vise and twisting the grip with pliers. A few pole grips—notably on Kerma's Corrective Angle poles—are glued on and are nearly impossible to remove.

Replace a grip by pushing it on as far as it will go and tap it home with a mallet.

To shorten a pole, remove the grip. Measure off the amount to be removed and score the aluminum shaft all the way around with the edge of a file. You can now hacksaw through the shaft or simply

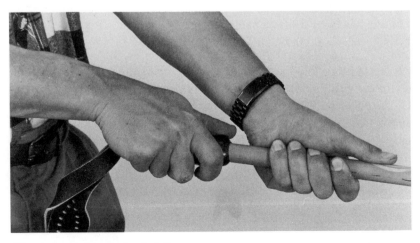

Remove a pole grip by twisting . . .

deepen the score and snap the end of the shaft off with a screwdriver. Use the file to smooth off the remaining jagged edge.

The steel points of ski poles are sometimes knocked loose and lost. Some ski shops sell replacement tips, which can simply be epoxied in place.

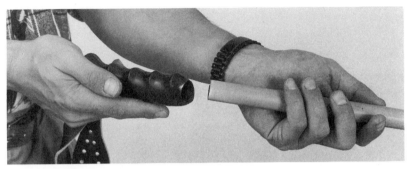

. . . and pulling.

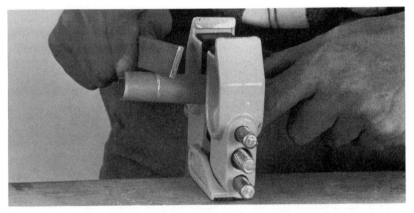

To shorten a pole, first score the shaft with the edge of a file . . .

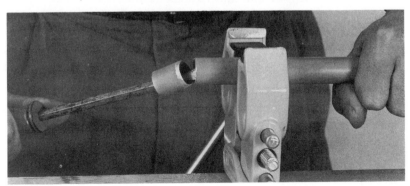

. . . and snap the end off with a screwdriver.

15
Goggles

The most common problem with goggles is scratched and cracked lenses. If your goggle lenses are damaged beyond repair and you can no longer find a replacement lens, drop in at a motorcycle shop and see if it stocks replacement lenses for your goggles. If not, buy a polycarbonate motorcycle face shield. Using your old, damaged lens as a pattern, cut out a replacement lens. Polycarbonate is tough stuff. You'll need a very sharp knife or a pair of small metal shears for the job.

Are your lenses continually popping out or peeling loose? Glue them in place with an automotive silicone sealer. It makes a good, flexible, waterproof bond and you can peel it off when it comes time to replace the lens.

Goggle straps can be repaired or replaced by anyone who knows how to use a sewing machine. Use a zigzag stitch to keep the elastic stretchy. Goggles worn over a racing helmet need extra-long straps. Most competition goggles are sold with long straps, but recreational goggles can be converted to helmet use by sewing in an extra piece of elastic material. Check first to make sure the goggle frames will fit under the helmet's face opening.

When the foam padding that rests against the face comes adrift, or the foam baffles that seal out the powder tear loose, glue them back with silicone sealer.

Many goggles can be customized to fit over eyeglasses simply by cutting notches in the frames to fit over the temple pieces of your specs. To keep your glasses from fogging inside the goggles, rub dishwashing liquid or hand soap on both sides of the lenses—both the eyeglass lenses and the goggle lenses—and polish them smooth with a soft cloth.

Appendix A: Glossary

Antifriction pad—A Teflon pad attached to the ski, usually via the toe unit of the binding, on which the toe of the boot rests. It is designed to reduce friction between the boot sole and the ski top, especially during forward-weighted twisting falls, historically the most dangerous kind of falls.

Base wax—A sealer wax, used for impregnating new ski bases and as a base for racing waxes.

Chatter—Instability of the ski, often caused by excessive vibration; usually most noticeable on very hard snow.

Concave—A ski base is said to be concave when the polyethylene base is dished lower than the hard steel edges. *Railing* is a similar condition.

Convex—A ski is said to be convex when the edges are worn down below the level of the polyethylene base.

Cracked edge—A type of one-piece steel edge with very narrow gaps machined partway through it. The purpose of the cracks is to minimize the influence of the springy steel edge on the ski's dynamic and flex characteristics. To compensate for the loss of edge stiffness, skis with cracked edges are normally thicker, which makes them both torsionally stiffer and damper (see *damping*). These are desirable characteristics for slalom racing skis, and many first-rate slalom skis have cracked edges.

Continuous edge—A one-piece steel edge with a smooth, uninterrupted contact length. The continuous steel edge is the strongest part of any ski. A continuous edge glides more quickly than a cracked edge, so giant slalom and downhill skis are built with continuous edges. Handmade racing skis used by top racers generally have very thin, rather fragile edges, which flex easily to maintain good contact with the snow and which maximize contact of the fast waxed base with the snow. The nonporous steel edge itself won't hold wax.

Damping—A ski's internal resistance to continued vibration. Most of a ski's damping influence is derived from its contact with the snow. In softer snow, especially in wet snow, continued vibration is a real advantage, since it helps break up water droplets under the base and improves glide. On very hard snow, however, uncontrolled vibration can lead to chatter and loss of edge grip. Good damping materials are those with high internal molecular friction—friction that dissipates energy as heat, instead of storing the impact energy and then springing back. Steel and aluminum are lively, or undamped, materials. Fiberglass and rubber are quiet, or damping, materials. Damping is most important for slalom skis on icy race courses. Most of the rubber used in metal sandwich skis is only intended incidentally for vibration damping: its real purpose is to provide a durable and flexible bond between the steel edges and the aluminum structural layers.

Extruded base—A ski running surface made of relatively soft polyethylene with a molecular weight of one million or less. It's manufactured by melting polyethylene powder and rolling it into a sheet. Extruded bases are dense, with lots of crystals in a softer matrix. They wear quickly but oxidize fairly slowly and are easy to grind and tune. P-tex 1000 is an extruded material.

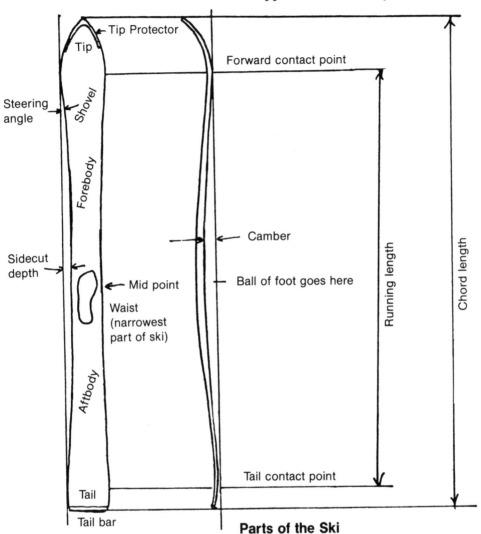

Parts of the Ski

Flex distribution—The pattern of stiffness along the length of the ski. Racing skis are generally stiffer than recreational skis, but there are also important differences in the balance of stiffness from shovel, to middle, to tail. For instance, most giant slalom skis are stiff in the middle and only moderately firm in the shovel and tail, while most slalom skis are moderately firm in the middle and quite stiff at the tail. A ski with forebody (section of ski before the boot) and afterbody (section of ski after the boot) that flex about equally is said to be balanced.

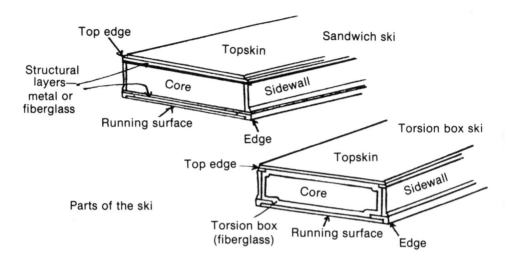

Parts of the ski

Flow—In boots, flow is the generic term for the thixotropic, puttylike materials used to provide an adaptable fit in some models. The flow softens under heat and pressure and conforms to the shape of the foot. It is normally contained in plastic bags sewn into the innerboot at critical fitting areas: over the instep (Hanson and some Lange boots) or around the ankle bones and sides of the feet (many Italian boots).

Hooky—Describes a ski that tends to continue turning while the skier is trying to get off the edge to start another turn.

Railing—When the ski's edges are extended beyond the level of the plastic running surface (see *concave*).

Release tension—The force that must be applied to a boot to release it from a binding. Release tension is adjustable, usually by turning a screw to preload a spring, which forces a bearing surface against a cam. Release tension can vary considerably since starting friction (the force required to get two contacting surfaces to start sliding over one another) is higher than sliding friction. Thus, in a slow twisting fall, where forces build up gradually, starting friction may never be overcome, in which case the binding will not release and injury may result. Binding manufacturers are at great pains to reduce starting friction for this reason, and this is also the reason it is vitally important to keep antifriction surfaces on boots and bindings clean and lubricated. In a fast fall the impact on the binding is usually more than sufficient to overcome starting friction. Force equals mass times velocity squared, so if you fall at twice the speed, you exert four times as much force on your bindings. The corollary is that the slower you ski, the less dependable your bindings may be.

Sandwich—A type of ski construction in which upper and lower structural members, normally sheets of aluminum or fiberglass, are glued to a core of wood, foam, or some composite material.

Shovel—The forward part of a ski, through the widest and thinnest section and up into the tip.

Sidecut—Viewed from directly above or below, all modern alpine skis have concave sides—they are narrow in the middle and broader at tip and tail. The shape of a ski's side curve is referred to as its *sidecut* (sometimes as its *side camber*). *Extreme* sidecut refers to a ski markedly narrower at the middle than at the ends. All else being equal, such a ski will initiate turns more abruptly, and carve a tighter turn, than a ski with a straighter, more moderate sidecut, where the difference between the waist width and the width at tip and tail is less extreme. While the waist is the narrowest part of the ski, the tail is normally narrower than the shovel.

Sintered base—A ski running surface made of hard polyethylene with a molecular weight of 1.5 million or more. It's manufactured by compressing polyethylene powder under tremendous pressure until the powder fuses together into a solid round block about four inches thick. After the block cools, a long thin sheet is skived off its edge, "uncoiling" the entire wheel. Material near the end of the sheet, from the center of the block, which cooled and cured more slowly, may sometimes make a faster running surface—there is some dispute on this point, but it is true that variations exist in the speed of skis equipped with "identical" sintered bases. P-tex 2000, 4000, and 6000, and HMW 3 and 5 are brand names for some sintered materials. In general, a higher molecular weight means the material is tougher, faster, and less dense. Lower density in turn means the plastic absorbs more wax. Sintered bases are low in crystalline content, stand up very well to rock damage, need to be waxed frequently to avoid oxidation, and hold their shape well between tunings.

Sidewall—The vertical side of the ski, usually armored with a plastic filler to protect the core from moisture and consequent warping and splitting. This filler is usually a very hard, dense material—phenol or ABS. Some skis, however, use an elastic sidewall of rubbery urethane, and in many injection-molded skis the foam core forms its own sidewall.

Stability—A ski that is not oversensitive to small irregularities in the snow, and therefore feels smooth and solid underfoot, is said to be stable.

Torsion—The resistance of a ski to being twisted along its length. A ski that is torsionally very stiff drives its edges at the shovel and tail into the snow more aggressively and may therefore steer very quickly. A ski that is torsionally soft tends to follow uneven terrain better. Metal sandwich skis tend to be torsionally stiff, and so do skis with cracked edges. A designer must carefully balance torsional stiffness against flex distribution and sidecut to achieve the steering quickness and terrain absorption he wants.

Torsion box—A form of ski construction in which a spacer core is enclosed in a box of stiff load-carrying material, usually a plastic resin reinforced with fiberglass. The outer box works as a monocoque structure, and its dynamic characteristics are controlled by varying its relative height, width, and wall thickness. Most torsion-box skis are made by wrapping the core in uncured, resin-soaked sheets of fiberglass and are therefore referred to frequently as *wet-wrap* skis or *glass-wrap* skis.

Tracking—The ability of a ski to hold a straight course on every type of snow.

Waist—The narrowest part of the ski, in plane view (looking directly down at the ski). In modern skis it is normally located near the heel of the boot.

Warp—A lateral twist or deformation in a ski. Warped skis can seldom be straightened permanently. New skis occasionally arrive slightly warped, and all skis should be checked periodically for warping. Warped skis should be replaced under warranty whenever possible.

Appendix B:
Troubleshooter's Guide

Problem	Possible Cause	How to Fix It
Skis won't hold on hard snow	Edges dull or rusted or base convex	File for flatness, edge-file
	Skis too soft or too short	Test better skis
	Bindings don't grip boot sole adequately	Check boot sole wear, binding adjustment
Skis unpredictable in turn initiation, wash out at beginning or end of turn, skip or buck when edged at high speed	Edges dull at tip and/or tail	File for flatness and edge-file, leaving skis sharp to tip and tail
	Bindings don't grip boot sole adequately	Check boot sole wear, binding adjustment
Skis hook, won't come off edge, or won't swivel in softer snow	Edges burred or too sharp at tip and tail	Dull edges at tip and tail, round off tail bar and tip protector
	Skis concave or railed	File for flatness
Skis bog down or slow abruptly, unpredictably, when passing from hard to soft snow or sun to shade	Wrong wax or no wax	Consult waxing chart and rub on appropriate wax
Skis slow, sticky	Wrong wax or no wax	Apply appropriate wax
	Bases badly gouged	Patch bases and flat file

Problem	Possible Cause	How to Fix It
Skis "rudder," refuse to turn in deep snow	Skis concave or railed	Flat-file
	Tails too stiff	Dull tails or use softer skis
	Skis too narrow	Use wider, softer skis
Skis turn better in one direction than the other	Skis warped or bent	Replace skis
	Edge of one ski badly burred	File for flatness, edge-file
	Binding loose on one ski	Check boot sole wear, binding adjustment
Skis unstable, wander apart; won't initiate turns quickly	Boots need canting	Install wedges with thick edge inboard
Skis contiually cross tips even on smooth terrain	Boots need coating	Install wedges with thick edges outboard
Skis feel heavy, long, awkward; won't turn easily	Skis concave or railed	Flat-file
	Foot pronates inside shell	Add custom-molded orthotic insole

Problem	Possible Cause	How to Fix It
	Boots too soft or too large	Test better boot
	Skis too long or too stiff	Dull tip and tail
Cold toes	Boots too tight over instep	Loosen instep buckle or remove insole
	Boots too tight around Achilles tendon	Remove foam padding from behind ankle pockets
	Boots stored wet overnight	Dry boot liners with hair dryer
	Boots leak	Seal toe dam with silicone sealer or tape; dry liner
Blisters	Boots too wide	Add padding to outside of innerboot
	Boots too long	Try smaller boot
Toes bruised under toenails; nail turns black	Boots too short	Buy longer boots or have shop enlarge boot toes
Muscle pain in thighs and lower back; mogul skiing too punishing	Boots too stiff	Soften boot flex
Unable to make proper forward-weighted turns; always sitting back	Inadequate forward lean	Add padding to back of innerboot, between innerboot and highback spoiler

Problem	Possible Cause	How to Fix It
Pressure points or painful hot spots	Boots too stiff	Soften boot flex
	Flow material badly distributed	Warm innerboots with hair dryer and knead flow out smooth
	Boot too tight over painful spot	Remove foam padding from innerboot at site of hot spot
Pain or cramps over instep	Boot too tight over instep	Remove insole or grind footbed thinner
Pain or cramps in arch or vamp of foot	Built-in arch support too high	Remove insole and grind arch support thinner or replace insole with orthotic
Bruised shins	Tongue deformed	Steam tongue, re-form it
	Tongue broken	Replace tongue or buy new boot
	Tongue too shoft	Reinforce back of tongue
	Shell too low and stiff	Reinforce back of tongue or soften shell flex
Shins rubbed raw	Tongue too sticky or abrasive	Tape plastic bag around tongue or spray with silicone

Problem	Possible Cause	How to Fix It
Bindings release too easily	Forward pressurre incorrect at heel	Check and adjust forward pressure at heel
	Release value set too low	Check and adjust release setting
	Release springs fatigued	Return to shop for replacement
Bindings don't return to center after lateral test	Forward pressure incorrect at heel	Check and adjust
	Toe-cup height set too low	Check and adjust
Bindings won't release in twist-out self-test	Heel-cup height set too low	Check and adjust
	Antifriction pad or toe-cup liners dirty, scored, or missing	Check condition and replace if necessary
	Dirt in sole of boot	Check and clean
	Binding unlubricated	Lubricate with silicone spray
	Too much snow packed under boot sole	Clean snow off boot sole and ski top
	Ice packed inside binding mechanism	Check and, if necessary, warm bindings to melt out ice

Problem	Possible Cause	How to Fix It
Boot won't enter binding or binding won't close	Too much snow packed under boot sole	Clean off snow
	Toe-cup height or heel-cup height incorrect	Check and adjust
	Forward pressure at heel incorrect	Check and adjust
	Heel-cup treadle broken	Return to shop for replacement
Bindings loose, rattling	Toe or heel cup incorrect height	Check and adjust
	Mounting screws stripped or loose	Check and repair screw placement
	Toe- or heel-cup adjustment screws stripped or missing, or pivot post bent	Return to shop for replacement

Appendix C: General Guide to Racing Wax Systems

Brand: Temperature		Toko World Cup			Swix Alpine	Hertel Hot Sauce	Fall Line Speed Wax
C°	F°	New snow	Man made snow	Old snow			
+15	+59				Yellow & Red		Orange
+10	+50	Red	Red	Yellow		Yellow	Red
+5 *Wet snow*	+41	Red & Green	Red	Yellow & Red	Red & Yellow	Red & Yellow / Red	
0 Freezing	+32		Red & Green		Red / Purple & Yellow	Red & Blue	Clear
−5 *Dry snow*	+23	Green & Red			Purple & White	Blue	Blue
−10	+14	Green	Green & Red		Purple / Blue & White		Green
−15	+5				Blue / Green & White		
−20	−4				Green		

Hertel Hot Sauce: White All-Temperature Wax (↕)

Holmenkol		Alpine Competition		Slik	U.S. Ski Wax	Vola	Kwik	Briko
Olympic Wax H3	Piste Racing	New snow	Old snow					
		Orange	Orange	Yellow	Paraffin & Red	Orange		
	Red	Red & Orange		Yellow & Red	Red		Red & Impregnation Wax	Orange
Yellow	Blue	Red / Red & Blue	Red & Orange	Red	Red & Blue	Blue	Red / Blue / Green	White
Red			Red	Red & Blue	Blue		Green & Hardener	
		Blue	Red & Blue	Blue	Blue & Green	Olive		Red
			Blue					
					Green			
White		Blue & Green / Green	Blue & Green / Green					

← Yellow All-Temperature Wax →

Appendix D: Grinding Grits for Base Structure

Use silicon carbide sandpaper in the following grades:

80 grit—For rough sanding, to flatten high spots and repair patches and to prepare skis for fine finish. Produces a hairy, rough surface. May also be used for final structure in high-speed racing (over 50 mph) in warm snow, at above-freezing temperatures.

100 grit—For final structure in high-speed racing in moderate temperatures (5° Fahrenheit to freezing).

180 grit—The standard finish grade. For final structure in slalom and giant slalom at moderate temperatures (5° to 32° Fahrenheit), and for downhill racing at very cold temperatures (below 5° Fahrenheit).

220 grit—For final structure in slalom and giant slalom at very cold temperatures.

Appendix E: Where to Find It

The following companies manufacture or import ski maintenance equipment and supplies. If your local ski shop doesn't stock an item you need, one of these firms can provide it.

Allstone Ski Tools, Inc.
2906 Pine Ave.
Niagara Falls, NY 14301
Tools and supplies.

Alpine Crafts Company, Inc.
PO Box 2467
South San Francisco, CA 94080
Vola ski wax, Supernaltene repair candles, files, and tools.

Collins Ski Products, Inc.
PO Box 11
Bergenfield, NJ 07621
Files and file holders.

Custom Manufacturing of Vermont
PO Box 256
Hinesburg, VT 05461
Waxes, tools, and supplies.

Daleboot USA
2150 S. 3rd West St.
Salt Lake City, UT 84115
Boot-fitting aids.

Diamond Machining Technology
85 Hayes Memorial Dr.
Marlborough, MA 01752
Diamond whetstones and files.

Flofit Corporation
PO Box 9012
Boulder, CO 80306
Boot-fitting aids.

Fontaine Metal Products
200 27th St.
Sacramento, CA 95816
Sanders and stone grinders.

Hertel and Company, Inc.
1100 B L'Avenida
Mountain View, CA 94043
Waxes, tools, supplies, and vises.

Imports International Sales, Inc.
8025 E. 40th Ave.
Denver, CO 80207
Files and scrapers.

Kwik Ski Products
PO Box 98906
Seattle, WA 98188
Waxes, files, scrapers, tools, and supplies.

Maxiglide Products, Inc.
PO Box 302
State College, PA 16801
Teflon-based waxless glide formula.

Montana Sport USA Ltd.
7770 E. Iliff Ave.
Denver, CO 80231
Tools and supplies.

Nafco Industries, Inc.
PO Box 1893
Carson City, NV 89702
Vises, tools, and supplies.

Olin Ski Company, Inc.
475 Smith St.
Middletown, CT 06457
Ski-tuning kits and tools.

Reliable Racing Supply
624 Glen St.
Glens Falls, NY 12801
Waxes, files, scrapers, tools, and supplies.

Ski Accessories Co.
7340 Highland Rd.
Pontiac, MI 48054
Waxes, files, scrapers, tools, and supplies.

Ski Kare, Inc.
PO Box 716
Berthoud, CO 80513
Files, tools, and supplies.

Ski-Tek International/Holmenkol
Pine Square
266 Pine St.
Burlington, VT 05401
Waxes, tools, and supplies.

Ski Tools, Inc.
5428 Wilson Dr.
Mentor, OH 44060
Tuning and repair equipment.

Swix Sport USA
261 Ballardvale St.
Wilmington, MA 01887
Waxes, tools, and supplies.

Technology and Tools
Box E, Route 30
Bondville, VT 05340
Waxes, files, tools, supplies, and boot-fitting aids.

The Tool Company of New Hampshire
PO Box 47, Route 106
Concord, NH 03301
Waxes, files, tools, and supplies.

Toko Div. of Uvex
10 Thurber Blvd.
Smithfield, RI 02917
Waxes, files, tools, and supplies.

Wintersport/Superfeet
Minaret Blvd.
Mammoth Lakes, CA 93546
Tools, supplies, and boot-fitting aids.

Index